The Dynamic Social Contract

An American Case Study

by
Andre L. Smith
Fayetteville State University

Series in Politics

VERNON PRESS

www.vernonpress.com

In the Americas:
Vernon Press
1000 N West Street, Suite 1200
Wilmington, Delaware, 19801
United States

In the rest of the world:
Vernon Press
C/Sancti Espiritu 17,
Malaga, 29006
Spain

Series in Politics

Library of Congress Control Number: 2022950721

ISBN: 978-1-64889-714-6

Also available: 978-1-64889-599-9 [Hardback]; 978-1-64889-657-6 [PDF, E-Book]

Table of Contents

List of Figures

List of Figures

List of Tables

List of Maps

Abstract

The social contract is explored as a dynamic sociopolitical instrument that is influenced by the context of human interactions, specifically, space. Space or proximity exists as a variable both increasing interactions and challenging sociopolitical norms or decreasing interactions and reinforcing sociopolitical norms. At its most seminal level, genetic connections cement communion within the social contract, but as space increases the context of connections becomes more abstract. As connections become more abstract, the social contract becomes dynamic or what Benedict Anderson (1983) describes as imagined. We can trace proximity within a sociopolitical model, with connections becoming more and more abstract as proximity increases and group membership becomes more abstract— global, global region, nation, religion, ethnicity, national region, city, town/village, and kin. We accept that kinship or hereditary connections are the most atomistic. And within this tree of proximity, as proximity increases the ties of group membership become more tenuous, and the incentive of collective action decreases Production is the binding glue of the world economic system, and the framework of the study, but it is within the bounds of the productive system that the challenge of proximity and membership collide. The collision occurs as proximity of production increases, and the reaction is a dynamic response within the social contract, witnessed as a retraction.

Introduction

They left untouched the old master-servant laws that were highly prejudicial to workers as well is laws that interpreted labor organizations as felonious conspiracies. Capitalism didn't eliminate oppressive upper classes. It just changed the basis upon which they stood. The ladders for social mobility were spread about the landscape more generously, but those without capital suffered as had those without inherited stasis earlier

Joyce Appleby

Charles Dickens began his famous novel *A Tale of Two Cities,* with the line, "It was the best of times and the worst of times." The line is prophetic when examining citizenship; specifically, within the context of social contract theory. Social contract theory provides a simple understanding of the social contract. Social contract theory in its most simplistic form establishes that people live together in society in accordance with an agreement that establishes moral and political rules of behavior. The question arises, what does it mean to be a citizen? Are there some who have more citizenship rights than others; simply, is there a duality of citizenship? The questions rest in both statutory definitions of citizenship and tacit norms of citizenship. For constitutional democracies, the definition of citizenship is generally defined: In the United States, the *Fourteenth Amendment, Section Two* reads,

> All persons born or naturalized in the United States, and subject to the jurisdiction thereof, are citizens of the United States and of the state wherein they reside. No state shall make or enforce any law which shall abridge the privileges or immunities of citizens of the United States; nor shall any state deprive any person of life, liberty, or property, without due process of law; nor deny to any person within its jurisdiction the equal protection of the laws.

Yet, this Amendment, which was ratified in 1868, preceded the sociolegal doctrine of "Separate but Equal," which effectively defined American citizenship through the lenses of skin color. The American Fourteenth Amendment defines "birthright" citizenship, if a person is born on American soil, that person is granted American citizenship. Additionally, if a person is born to American citizens, that person is granted American citizenship. The history of United States citizenship is not an anomaly in world history: In 1842, the newly unified Germany defined citizenship as a birthright, *jus sanguinis*, of German decent (Pautz, 2005); The Japanese Nationality Law of 1950 follows the *jus sanguinis* format and enlists a strenuous process for naturalization (Lee, 2011). The examples are of statutory laws that define citizenship via the lenses of land and hereditary; you are born on the land or of others from the land.

At its most seminal level, citizenship is the paramount maxim of the social contract. The social contract, which can be understood as a tacit agreement among individuals through which organized society is brought into existence. Yet, from the preceding examples, the social contract can be formally and informally exclusive, allowing citizenship privileges to others and simultaneously denying it to others. Within the scope of citizenship, let us utilize a description of Western citizenship provided by Peter Riesenberg (1992): citizenship is a form of exchange among privileged members.[1] It is a simple description echoed by three political philosophers that offered the most succinct explanations of the social contract and citizenship, Thomas Hobbes, John Locke, and Jean-Jacques Rousseau. The three philosophers differ on their positions regarding the political spectrum, but all share a key similarity in their belief that there should exist a contract of supreme power, government, that exists to administer the rights of man, citizens, the privileged members.

Figure 1.1: Group Membership, expanding from familial to global affiliation.

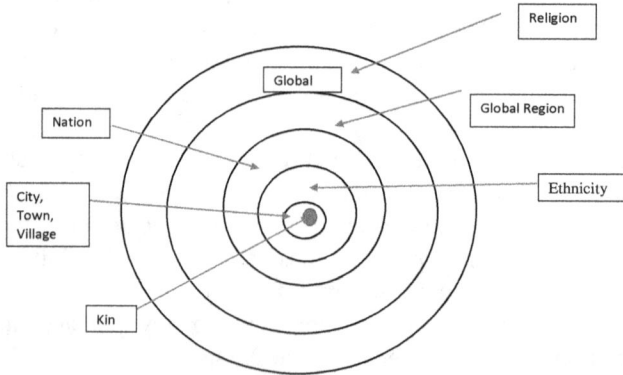

---

[1] Aristotle provides the first Western synthesis of citizenship, but the definition is intimately related to Aristotelian virtue. He defines moral virtue as a disposition to behave in the right manner and as a mean between extremes of deficiency and excess, vices. Aristotle synthesizes virtue within citizenship, with a definition of citizenship as a person who possesses the virtues of ruling and being ruled. Therefore, a noncitizen is an individual who does not have or is incapable of virtue.

For simplicity of argument, let us agree that in organized societies some form of a social contract exists and has existed for millennia, and that at its most seminal base the unit of analysis is membership within the group, citizenship. We can further delineate group membership from the tree: global, global region, nation, religion, ethnicity, national region, city, town/village, kin. The tree becomes more expansive as we move up, and conversely, personal connections become sparser as illustrated in *Figure 1.1.* Following group membership to its most basic organizing level, kinship, we can define the kinship connection as the most personal, and global as the most impersonal.

Membership is the binding glue of social contract theory. It is what gives locus to collective identity and action, and it defines access and privilege. At the kinship level, it is simply defined as shared hereditarian lineage, but it becomes more complicated as we move along the tree of membership. At the national level, we can define membership as citizenship within the context of Roman citizenship: citizenship in ancient Rome was a privileged and legal status afforded to free individuals. The privileges of Roman citizenship included: *Lus suffagii*: the right to vote; *Lus honorum*: the right to stand for civil public office; and *Lus commercii*: the right to make legal contracts and to hold property. In the Western world, Enlightenment thinkers coalesced the abstract of Roman citizenship into the concept of liberalism. Liberalism embraces individuality, which holds that given intellectual freedom, individuals/groups will develop institutions into "pareto optimizing" systems. Institutions that exist only in political/socio environments where individuals practice suffrage, exercise the freedom to join or construct public institutions, and can join and/or be bounded by legal rights and contracts, rules. Samuel Beer (2006, p. 695) gives a parsimonious explanation of liberalism: "According to liberal doctrine, the reason men should be free to govern themselves is that they can think for themselves."

Let us define membership as citizenship, nationalism, within the context of liberalism. We witness within this context of membership that personal connections become scarcer. Yet, there are shared identities connected by concepts of sovereignty. Benedict Anderson (1983, p. 6) describes this shared identity, "It is *imagined* because the members of even the smallest nation will never know most of their fellow-members, meet them, or even hear them, yet in the minds of each lives the image of their *communion.*" The communion weakens as we move from national to global; even imagined connections do not exist outside of shared religions at the global level. Therefore, at the global level the binding glue of the social contract becomes non-existent or marginal, but even within the national sphere, the social contract is not static but predicated on abstract notions of shared fate.

Let us declare that the social contract is not static but is bounded by dynamic institutional constraints. North's (1990, p. 4) definition of institutions clarifies the bounds of a dynamic social contract: "Institutions include any form of constraint that human beings devise to shape human interaction." Thus, institutions act to minimize the costs of interactions and, "…[constrain] …what individuals are prohibited from doing and, sometimes, under what conditions some individuals are permitted to undertake certain activities (North, 1990, 4)." Let us clarify that at its most atomistic level that the social contract is an institution, societies' most basic institution, which we will define as both informal and formal rules that bound human interactions (North, 1990).

Let us explore the rationale of the social contract as a means of shared survival via collective action. The logic of collective action is based in scarcity, a scarcity of resources (Ostrom, 1990). Resources are by nature scarce, and human survival is and has been about managing scarcity. Collective action increases survivability by decreasing transaction costs. A band of hunters is more likely to locate and bring down a large game than a lone hunter, and if one hunter is injured or killed, the loss to the hunting group is not catastrophic. The amount of food (game or crops) is scarce and dictated by natural and human forces: draught, natural disaster, disease, and other humans.

Cementing loyalty or in-group participation can be illogical. It may involve the suppression of self-interest for group interest, altruism. In a simple logic game, individual 1, is a member of group A. Group A is attacked by members of group B, which outnumber and are better armed. A logical choice is for individual 1 is to defect to group B; his/her odds of survival are greater with defection. Conversely, defection decreases the odds of group A's collective survival. Thus, what incentivizes individual 1 to act against his/her own self-interest for collective group survival. For the most atomistic group, it is kinship connections, which we will define as the base level of personal connectivity.

The question arises, outside of kinship connections what incentivizes collective action? John Locke (1687) presented the classical response, which is based on pure self-interest. Locke (1687) wrote within the context of collection action:

> …though in the state of nature he has such a right, yet the enjoyment of it is very uncertain and constantly exposed to the invasion of other. For all being kings as much as he, every man his equal, and the greater part no strict observers of equity and justice, the enjoyment of the property he has in this state very unsafe very unsecure. This make him willing to quit this condition, which, however free, is full fears and continual dangers: and it is not without reason that he seeks out and is

willing to join in society with others who are already united, or have a mind to unite, for the mutual preservation of their lives, liberties, and estates, which I call by the general name *property* (Second Treatise).

Thus, it is within man's self-interest to collectively act with others to secure himself from the dangers of "nature" or other men.

The locus of collective action was further explored within the context of self-interest via the rational choice framework, which has origins in economic theory. Russell Hardin (1971) presented a model of individual behavior based on self-interested rational choice. That collective action is a simple maximalization of utilities. The logic is that the self-interested individuals will recognize mutual group interest and will tailor behavior to maximize group objectives, which will result in the maximization of individual utility. Hardin's (1968) "herder game" provides the classical example of recognized self-interest. The game, the prisoner's dilemma, conceptualization requires that all players are given complete information:

> Suppose we think of the players in a game as being herders using a common grazing meadow. For this meadow, there is an upper limit to the number of animals that can graze on the meadow for a season and be well fed at the end of the season. We call that number I. For a two-person game, the "cooperate" strategy can be thought of as grazing I./2 animals for each herder. The "defect" strategy is for each herder to graze as many animals as he thinks he can sell at a profit (given his private costs), assuming that this number is greater than I.2. If both herders limit their grazing to I./2, while the other grazers as many as he wants, the "defector" obtains 11 units of profit, and the "sucker" obtains – 1. If each chooses independently without the capacity to engage in a binding contract, each chooses his dominant strategy, which is to defect. When they both defect, they obtain zero profit (Ostrom 1990, p. 4).

If we follow, that individuals do not always act in their own self-interest without coercion, what is the most common form of coercion? In the above example, it was monetary gain. It is a given that in a totalitarian environment that fear is the chief component to push individuals to act against their own self-interest. Outside of coercion, it is a perceived communion of collective interest that cements collective action (Anderson, 1983). It is a communion of connectiveness cemented by shared history, language, religion, or ethnicity. Let us reframe the tree of collective groups and reorder the connections as proximity, specifically, living spaces. Let us argue that as proximity increases, the incentive of collective action decreases.

The Constrained Social Contract

The social contract is constrained and dynamic. The philosophical manifestation of the social contract is a collective bounded by *shared* morality. Historically, the social contract has been exclusive and dynamic. Let us begin with the latter, the dynamic nature of the social contract. Scarcity sets the bounds of the social contract. During periods of scarcity, the collective or communal nature of the social contract is amplified. Survival during periods of scarcity dictates a reliance on personal connections for mutual survival. Individualism, liberalism, is checked during periods of scarcity as the calculus of survival is communal. Conversely, during periods of surplus the dynamics of the social contract expands as individualism or liberalism is more freely accepted. An example of the latter was the historical movement from feudalism to industrialization. The transformation witnessed the lessoning of the communal nature of survival, as individual survival became less dependent on neighbors and kinship connections.

The exclusivity of the social contract is as elemental as the primary kinship incentive of collective action. The first incentive to act collectively without defection is kinship. Logically, the absence of kinship bonds disincentivized loyalty and increased defection; as collectives or communities became more heterogenous, personal connections became more complex, but remained central to communal standing. The communal nature of the social contract advanced from kinship, ethnicity, region, faith, and nationalism. The organizing basis of the Western feudalistic social contract was shared faith. Faith outside the Roman Catholic religion or excommunication excluded one from the rights of the faithful; however, conversion was a means of gaining the exclusive rights of membership or privileges.

The historical end of Western feudalism challenged the glue of the social contract, shared faith. The exclusive nature of the social contract expanded within a framework of nationalism and skin color. Carole Pateman (1988) explored the paternalistic nature of the Western social contract and its gender-exclusive nature, with her description of the "sexual" social contract. Charles Mills (1997) expanded Pateman's discourse within the exclusive skin color nature of the Western social contract, which they both expanded into a wider discourse of gender and racial discrimination with their joint 2007 exploration, *Contract and Domination.*

The Model

The Framework: The framework for this examination is grounded in systems theory. World systems analysis is about the analysis of how we conceptualize social change (Wallerstein 2004). It is analogous to the exploration as it examines the dynamic transformations of the social contract and counter responses. The model of the social contract presented is both dynamic and exclusive. It is dynamic as it transforms during periods of surplus and is exclusively connected to "imagined" collective communions (Anderson, 1983). Each dynamic transformation of the social contract is met by an equal response, with perceived or real decreases in personal connections. Karl Polanyi (1944) described this reaction as the "Double Movement," which we will identify as the peasant/laborer response to the transformation of feudalism to industrialization. It is within this context of citizenship that we witness of reformulation of the "feudal social contract" which we will identify for simplicity's sake as "communal" to the modern which we will simplify identity as "transactional." It is the genesis of this reformulation of the sociopolitical order that is the theme of this exploration.

The second aspect of the systems analysis framework is the classification of historical world systems based on means of production. Immanuel Wallerstein (2004) argues that the historical and present world systems where and/are organized by their modes of production. It relies on a materialistic conceptualization as the basis of society, which we define as surplus and scarcity.[2] World societies have historically been organized within three modes of production: mini-system; world-empire, and world economy (Wallerstein 2004; Bartley et al. 2000). The *mini-system* is the reciprocal-linage mode of production, which is based on very limited specialization of tasks and production based on hunting, gathering, and rudimentary agriculture. Mini systems are small kinship bands with the basic organization principle of age and gender (Flint and Taylor, 2011).

The world-empire system mode of production consists of large groups of agricultural producers who produce a minimal surplus. The surplus allows for the development of specialized non-agricultural producers, artisans and administrators. The production between the agricultural producers and the artisans is reciprocal, but the distinguishing factor is the appropriation of the agricultural surplus by the administrators. The administrators utilize the surplus to form a bureaucratic ruling class or elite. This system has appeared historically in countless political iterations, and cements material inequality not found in mini systems, as material gains are pushed upward to elites

---

[2] "This is much broader concept than the orthodox Marxist definition in that it includes not only the way win which productive tasks are divided up but also decisions concerning the quantities of goods to be produced, their consumption and/or accumulation, and the resulting distribution of goods" (Flint and Taylor 2011, p.14).

(Wallerstein, 2004). Examples of empire systems were the Roman Empire and Western Feudalism.

The final world system is the *world-economy*, which is based on the capitalist mode of production. The criterion of the world-economy system is production and profitability, and the primary drive of the system is the accumulation of surplus capital. There is no hierarchal political structure or ideology, only liberalized market ideology. Competition between different units of production is solely market-driven with less efficient producers destroyed by the more efficient.

Immanuel Wallerstein (2004) argues that the mini and empire systems of production were fragile were the world-economy system has been robust. Wallerstein contends that after the mid-fifteenth century that capitalism robustly expanded throughout Western Europe to eventually encapsulate the entire globe. It is within this world-system that binds our framework of active responses within the dynamic social contract. It is the capitalistic necessity of constant profit growth that pushes the proximity of production and consumption further apart, which is the basics of the loss of the "imagined" community (Anderson, 1983). Thus, the world-economy consists of a single market, capitalism. Production is simply for exchange rather than use; producers do not consume but trade within the world market for the best prices.

The Dependent & Independent Variables: The social contract, in its many historical iterations, is the conceptualized dependent variable. The examination utilizes brief historical and empirical analysis of social transformations, which we theorize as dynamic changes within the social contract. The locus or proximity of production is a conceptualized measure of personal connections, and as production and consumption geographical proximity increases conversely the bounds of the social contract constrict. Simply, as personal connections become sparse, the social contract becomes more exclusive.

Within the language of the *world-system* framework, elitism moved from the simple bounds of hereditarian aristocracy (*empire*) to incorporate the bourgeoisie as the calculus of wealth transformed from land to capital. The peasant transformed from the communal to the transaction-based laborer, the proletariat; and the full jeopardy of survival was fully rested with the anonymous individual. The burgeoning socioeconomic order was jeopardized by the expansive jeopardy of the laborer, as labor and community became more impersonal, and labor's awareness of the jeopardy coalesced into a counter response, which Karl Marx (1867) coined as "class struggle."

The twentieth and twenty-first centuries witnessed increased globalized production and trade, and the response has been an inward retreat to manifestations of earlier historical *communions*: nationalism, racism, and xenophobia. If we operationalize this dynamic transactional social contract, we can identify proximity of production and consumption as the independent variable.

The layout of the examination is an American social, economic, and political case study. It begins with a historical preview of the theory, the genesis of the first transformation and the social contract. We follow with an examination of the gender and racial exclusive nature of the social contract. The third chapter examines the modern urban genesis and communal networks of American urbanization and the first reaction to the transactional contract. The fourth chapter examines the American labor movement and its attachment to the communal contract. The fifth chapter explores the effects of the transglobal contract within the United States and the world economic system, and the sixth and final chapter defines the American racial contract within the bounds of proximity.

Chapter 1

The Communal Social Contract

"This city is what it is because our citizens are what they are."

Plato

For Hobbes, man exists in a duality. A duality of a constant craving of power, which manifests as a natural state of war. The social contract acts as a regulator to maintain mans' existence. Hobbes (1651) wrote:

> ...the final cause, or end design of men (who naturally love liberty, and dominion over others) in the introduction of that restraint upon themselves (in which we see them live in commonwealths) is the foresight [prospect] of their own preservation and of more contented life thereby, that is to say, of getting themselves out from that miserable condition of war which is necessarily consequent (as has been shown) to the natural passions of men, when there is no visible power to keep them in awe and tie them by fear of punishment to the performance of their covenants and observation of those laws of nature... (Leviathan, 1651, Pt. 2 Ch. 17 s. 1).

John Locke, in a similar vein, believed that the social contract provided man protection from the violence of the natural world, and that the protection manifested as liberty. For Locke, the law was not a restriction upon mans' freedom but rather a tool to grant liberty. Locke (1687, p. 56) wrote:

> ... the end of law is not to abolish or restrain, but to preserve and enlarge freedom: for in all the states of created beings capable of laws, where there is no law, there is no freedom: for liberty is, to be free from restraint and violence from others.

Thus, man is so vulnerable in the state of nature, laws are created to establish mans' natural rights (property).

> ... if he [man] be absolute lord of his own person and possessions, equal to the greatest, and subject to nobody, why will he part with his freedom?... To which it is obvious, that though in the state of nature he has such a right,

yet the enjoyment of it is very uncertain and constantly exposed to the invasion of others... This makes him willing to quit a condition... that he seeks out, and is willing to join in society with others, who are already united, or have a mind to unite, for the mutual preservation of their... property (Second Treatise, Ch. 9 s. 123).

Jean-Jacques Rousseau follows the underlying logic of Locke and Hobbes, but his rationale is basic survival. For Rousseau, man cannot survive in the natural state, and the common good (survival) requires compulsion. The social contract, compulsion, secures mans' rights, "... whoever refuses to obey the general will shall be compelled to do so by the whole body (Rousseau, 1762, Ch. 7)." Thus, man will be forced to be free, and the condition of citizenship secures man against all personal dependence.

Hereditarian Foundations of Elitism

The historical norm of political institutions has been the maintenance of concentrated hereditarian power networks. The disaggregation of power within political institutions has only been short-term, and the cumulative nature of the concentrated system is bounded and even expanded by a dominant world economic system and a social contract based on hereditarian membership in the dominant political class.

A sociological historical glimpse of the collective behavior of humans witnessed a banding together for mutual survival, the *mini system*. The mutual survival of individuals increased with collective behavior, agricultural and hunting and gathering. The collective bands centered upon familial relations, which grew to tribal formulations that adhered to close familial ties. Surpluses in production increased connections across collective bands. Entrepreneurs managed the surplus to establish and maintain hereditary social classes; leaving only the "commons" for classes of individuals defined by social order (Ostrom, 1990). The entrepreneurs utilized tribal connections to coalesce and maintain larger bands and territories, but always maintaining a social class structure based on hereditary. Influence grew, and the sociopolitical structure grew to what Wallerstein (2004) described as empire, connections bounded by territory, land.

It was the profound nature of "empire" and reliance on familial social rules, institutions, that reinforced political norms. Political norms that reinforced control of territory, and control of territory was reinforced by the control and flow of surplus production. Collective action was dually mobilized for the twofold use of surplus production: the collective mechanizations of militarized bands and continued production of surplus to maintain militarized bands. The maintenance of militarized bands increased the capture of further territory and the collective bands of humans that inhabited territory.

The capturing of territory increased production and the expansion of familial social structures. Institutions developed to reinforce the "mechanisms" of empire, but at its heart was territory. The bounds of territory were the technological constraints of production. For most of human history, the bounds of unmechanized agrarian production bounded human population expansion and territorial encroachment. Human population constrained by production remained relatively constant until the expansion of the industrial revolution. Limited human population and territory constrained "empire" and required static adherence to the hereditary sociopolitical order (Appleby, 2010).

The institutional history of collective humanity centered on territory and a hereditarian-defined social order or a social contract. Social scientist can historically view the expansion of the republican city states within the Greek peninsula, twenty-six-hundred years ago, as a seminal challenge to the hereditarian-defined social order, but membership within the polis was defined by birthright. For ancient Athens, who practiced direct democracy, the vote or voice, was limited to adult men of direct lineage to other adult male Athenians (Bryce, 1929).

A republican representative democracy grew across the Aegean Sea on the nearby Italian peninsula. But within the representative democracy the social contract was buttressed by hereditary relations. The nationalism of empire and Roman citizenship was bounded by hereditary, and within the system, the political social order was buttressed by familial relations. The Roman ruling class was monopolized by a hereditary social order which held the bonuses of "empire" and political power within a patriarchal system with the patricians at its head, the plebeians in the middle, and non-Romans at its floor.

The seminal hereditarian social contract was not limited within Western European history but was the norm of collective human civilizations. The historical norm of hereditary dynasties can be traced from Asia, the African continent, and to the Eurasian peninsula. The cradle of civilization rests within the territory of the African Sahara. Dynastic civilizations flourished for thousands of years in the region before the rise of the Roman civilization. These civilizations culminated with the millennial stability of the Egyptian empire, which political social order was based on a hereditary social order.

The locus of empire and its reliance on a hereditarian-defined social contract extended throughout human civilization. The Shang dynasty rose in modern-day China about 1050 B.C. It relied on the locus of "empire" bounded by a hereditarian social order that mechanized the surpluses of human production to incapsulate swaths of territory into one expansive territory of political influence. The uniqueness of Chinese institutions was the creation of bureaucratic institutions influenced by the philosophy of Confucius, which delineated bureaucratic administration across hereditary classes within the first merit-based civil services institutions[1]. However, the social order and by extension the social contract remained static with surpluses of production unequally distributed within an aristocratic hereditarian class.

The genesis of political institutions in Western Europe can be traced as concessions of the hereditary elite within the constraints of the feudal system. A system bounded by the use and control of land. Within the system, a sociopolitical class structure existed that attached the lowest class as extensions of the land, and utilizing a familiar game metaphor, chess; the lowest social class, the peasants, were simply pawns. It is within this political system that the seminal Western social contract develops. It is a social contract defined by membership within the community of the faithful.

The binding glue of the feudal system was membership within the Roman Catholic faith. It was the primary sociopolitical institution of the feudal system and defined the rules of sociopolitical life. If one was excluded from the community, one was no longer bound to the sociopolitical benefits of membership and conversely could be treated as a "savage." The social contract buttressed and sustained the hereditarian benefits of class. The dogmatic concept of divine rule arises as a construct within the ruling institutions of the feudal systems and constrains "power" to a concentrated hereditary elite.

One was born a peasant or a nobleman, there was no means of climbing the social class ladder. The system provided unequal benefits to the hereditarian elite. Control of the land was the means of accessing wealth because people were attached to the land. The peasant worked the land and provided their surplus production to the hereditarian elite, absent conquest from a rival nobleman seeking expansion of their lands or excommunication.

The sociopolitical hereditarian institutionalization of the concentration of power was not solely synonymous with the West but was the norm of worldwide sociopolitical institutions. If we examine the sixth-century Islamic schism into its two main sects, Sunnis and Shia, excluding later developing differences in liturgy was leadership succession bounded by familial claims. Thus, the concept of dynastic succession is a prominent institutional element of pre-modern societies across geographies and ethnicities and the locus of *empire*.

---

[1] The bureaucratic merit system was based on gender exclusivity. It was only open to men.

For simplicity, a brief glimpse into Western institutions provides an enlightening example of the rigidity of the hereditarian aggregation of power and the retooling of hereditary into a broader social contract. English history provides a key example of intercessional conflict, between the concentrated hereditarian empowered elites with the 1215 *Magna Carta Libertatum*. The basis of the treaty was conflict between the hereditary nobleman and the hereditarily empowered monarch, King John. The result was a legal document, brokered by the Roman Catholic Church, which followed the legal strictures of the feudalistic social contract and reinforced the feudal system. The rebelling nobleman was ensured elite rights within the contract, the church reaffirmed its role as the atomistic sociopolitical institution, and the king was admonished for his extreme collection of surpluses "rents/taxes" from his fellow elites. The Magna Carta is held as a legal precursor to the political concept of liberalism, but the document simply recemented the existing social contract. There was only one class of people with defined legal rights, the aristocrats.

The Western Social Contract Rebranded

However, the 1648 conclusion of the Wars of Reformation was one of three sociopolitical movements that resulted in a retooling of the Western social contract and the Western conceptualization of citizenship. The second was the rise of capitalism spurred dually by the collapse of usury bans and the rise of limited liability corporations, and the third was technological advancement that freed a majority of the population from rural communal crop production to urban wage earners. The bounds of Roman Catholic Church were removed, and the social contract was reformulated within the bounds of Westphalian nationalism and navigation or interactions between citizens entered a state of transactional economic norms dictated by the bounds of the reformed social contract. No longer did a person residing in Paris solely consider themselves a member of the Catholic church or a subject of their respective monarch, they were a citizen of Paris; however, their wellbeing was no longer the purview of the landed lord, the majority of the citizens of Western Europe moved from the peasantry to the proletariat. The movement from the agricultural to the modern urban system was predicated on the production of food, which was witnessed by the static nature of human population for most of human existence.

Human population has and is bounded by crop production and disease. The formula of man hours to crop production is the model that has dictated human existence. It is a formula of scarcity. The onus of ancient societies to empower the landed local elite was the securing of the means to monitor the growing, selling, and exporting of food stuffs to lessen the threats of famine; for most of human history, the labor formula required that 80 percent of the population labor in agriculture to provide food for the population (Appleby, 2010). A large proportion of the population willingly labored within a communal social contract for mutual survival. The notion of industry was foreign, and most production took place within the home. The local and national exportation of food stuff was rigidly controlled, and the control was willingly given to landed elites. Because at the base level, survival was the foremost goal, and survival was tied to geographic proximity to others.

Technology remained static for millennia. If one could construct a hypothetical snapshot of agricultural production, one would notice that for thousands of years, human agricultural production remained technologically static. A hypothetical snapshot of an Italian farmer laboring in the fields during the first century would look remarkably similar to a farmer laboring in the same field fifteen-hundred years later. For thousands of years, farmers realized that livestock manure, fertilizer, increased crop yields, but this practice alone would still after several seasons leave acres of farmland nutrient poor. And the most common practice to regenerate nutrient-exhausted soil was the fallowing of fields for years as livestock crazing and its byproducts of wastes brought nutrients back to overused soil. The practice left thousands of acres of farmland unutilized for years, and limited production yields.

Within the agricultural model, the natural perils of drought, plight, and swarms of overconsuming insects were a recurring hazard, as they are today, but more disastrous for a tenuous system of agricultural production. A second issue was the limitations of food storage. Modern refrigeration and preservatives allow for the global shipment and preservation of food, but historically there were two methods of preserving food for the long winter months, drying, and fermentation. The limitations were the key factors that ensured that food production remained a local industry and minimally commercial.

Added to the limitations of agriculture was the threat of famine and disease. A local drought or plight equaled starvation and hovering equally with the fear of famine was the real threat of disease. Only two-hundred years ago (in 1800) 43 percent of children died before their fifth birthday (Chamberlain, 2006). And only one hundred years ago, in 1900 America, the three leading causes of death were pneumonia, tuberculosis, diarrhea, and enteritis (Center for Disease Control, 1999). The catastrophic consequences of ancient disease was the fourteenth century's "black death," which resulted in the death of fifty-million Europeans or sixty percent of the population. The disease culled the world population, which did not recover for another hundred years.

The constant threats of nature and the limitations of food production cemented the communal nature of the feudal social contract. The calculus of the social contract was the reliance on fellow citizens for survival. Communal crop production was the means of mutual survival. Peasants labored to grow the crops and shepherd the livestock. A percentage of the produced crops was kept sustaining family units, and the others were the tax paid to the landed lord.

The commercial limits of the practice were the command style of crop pricing. Local landed lords or boards set prices, which disincentivized the commercialization of agriculture. Overall, it maintained a system of control wherein the aristocracy monitored the growing, selling, and exportation of grain (Appleby, 2010, p. 5). The system managed scarcity and thereby managed unrest. The peasant willingly entered and maintained the feudal social contract to navigate the ever-present hazards of famine and disease, and the landed lord provided a reprieve in the extreme examples of the English "poorhouse."

Beginning in the sixteenth century, specifically, in Britain large increases in agricultural output began to challenge the outlines of the communal social contract. The output increases were directly related to farming techniques and policy change: enclosure, four-field crop rotation, and selective breeding. The definition of enclosure is to seal off an area with an artificial barrier, fence or wall. The common pre-sixteenth-century practice was open communal space, the commons. British farmers planted their crops on small strips of land and allowed their livestock to graze on the common fields. The open fields were part of the collective and were managed by the landed elites.

Consolidation of smaller land parcels became the norm in seventeenth-century Britain. Economic and technological change pushed by increased yields due to crop rotation; the physical enclosure of livestock on selected parcels, which brought nutrients to the soil in the form of nitrogenous waste products, and the easing of restrictions on the transport and sell of crops dually challenged the existing social order, communal social contract. The increases in production relaxed the eighty percent proportion of agriculture labor necessary to feed the populace.

Other socioeconomic and political changes were either localized in Britain or directly affected Britain; all were changes that would foster the transformation of the communal nature of the social contract in the Western world. The current world order is predicated upon capitalism, and capitalism does not function without the flow of capital. The logic of capital flow is interest, one is compensated for the use of one's capital. Simply, the borrower pays a fee over the sum that was borrowed for the use of monetary funds. The two dominant world religions of the seventeenth century viewed the practice of interest payments as immoral, and distinctly classified the practice as usury. In contrast to the principle of interest loans, are non-interest loans whereby loans are provided to the borrowers without charging interest on the principal. Moehlman (1934) cited Christian biblical verses to conclude that within the early Jewish community, there was a strict prohibition against charging interest on loans within the community (Exo. 2.25; Deut. 23.20-21). In fact, one of the first tenets of the formally organized Catholic church was to prohibit loan interest: The First Council of Nicaea forbade interest charging among Catholic clergy (Moehlman, 1934).[2] A principle that was later extended to the entire laity.

The prohibition on usury was a fundamental tenet of Catholic orthodoxy, as voiced by Thomas Aquinas. Aquinas viewed interest as a "double-charge" and a sin (Geisst, 2013). For Aquinas, the natural essence of money was a measure of value or intermediary in exchange. The increase of money through usury violated this essence; therefore, a just transaction was one characterized by an equality of exchange, one where each side received exactly his due (Moehlman, 1934; Geisst, 2013). Within a Thomistic analysis, interest payments of a loan in excess of the principle borrowed is a violation of the balance or equilibrium between borrower and lender and is therefore unjust. The heretical nature of usury was officially codified in 1179 with the *Third Council of the Lateran*.[3]

The unlawfulness of interest payments was codified into English law with the passage of the 1275 *Statute of the Jewry*, which both outlawed the practice of charging interest and was a thinly veiled anti-sematic assault on Jewish merchants and citizens. It signified that people of Jewish decent resided outside the realms or protections of the social contract, which was bound by membership within the Catholic faith.[4] It solidified the precommercial state of the Western world, which was challenged by technological and sociopolitical changes.

The English prohibition against loan interest was challenged during the sixteenth century. In 1545, Henry VIII passed the *Act Against Usurie*, (37 Hen. VIII. C. 9). The act was crucial in legalizing interest payments, which were essential to mercantilist imperialism. The English government created limited

---

[2] The prohibition against interest payments was codified into initial church canon in Nicaea but was later extended beyond the institutional realm to cover all Catholic laity.
[3] The Catholic Church heretical codification of interest continued into the eighteenth century with Pope Benedict XIV issuing an encyclical, *Vix Pervenit*, which reaffirmed the church's strong stand against the practice.
[4] Hundreds of Jews were arrested and executed. They were charged with usury, which was linked to blasphemy. Their property was seized by the crown, and in 1290 with the passage of the Edict of Expulsion all Jews were expelled from Britain with their property seized by the state. To avoid property confiscation and deportation many Jews converted to Christianity; thus, entering within the bounds of the feudal social contract.

liability corporations under royal charters and parliamentary acts to grant monopolies over specified colonial territories. In 1600, Queen Elizabeth I granted an exclusive right to trade with all countries to the east of Africa's Cape of Good Hope to the British East India Company. The East India Company was a limited liability corporation that sold stock or ownership shares. Shareholders risked their capital in the hope that the company would profit, which would result in owners' equity, dividend payments. The company worked intimately with the British government.

There were two methods of raising funds to cover the East India Company's colonial expansions, loans and stock offerings. The company practiced both capital raising techniques, with their unique risks. The issuing of stock potentially devalued existing stockholder shares and potentially could diminish dividend, profit, payments. A loan required revenue to pay interest, with a threat of default; however, the sixteenth century witnessed a dramatic drop in interest rates from the highs of around 20-30 percent to 9-10 percent (Marino, 1993). This spurred commercial enterprises that were again prompted by technological and sociopolitical change. Yet before we can coalesce these into the three socioeconomic factors that spurred a transformative change in the Western socioeconomic system, we must highlight the political change that gave an umbrella of protection to the transformation.

The feudal system was challenged by the Wars of Reformation, which resulted in the retooling of the social contract.[5] The Wars of Reformation began in the sixteenth century as a challenge to Roman Catholic Church corruption spurred by a reformist German monk, Martin Luther. The resultant generation-long conflict culminated with a sociopolitical umbrella that gave rise to the modern Western system, which we can trace to the end of the conflict, in 1648. The war ended with the treaty of Westphalia in 1648, which defined state sovereignty outside the bounds of external religious affiliation. States were defined as geographically contiguous areas bounded by common language and culture. States would practice sovereignty, governance, within its borders without the fear of external influence. Thus, by definition, a state exists when it exhibits control over the inhabitants that reside within its borders. And vice versa, citizens define themselves as members of the state by tacitly agreeing to submit to the collective bounds (governance) of the state, which we can define as citizenship (Bentley, 1949).

---

[5] The first fissure in the system was a rejection of feudal obligations at the highest tier. In 1533, King Henry VIII rejected papal authority and established the Church of England.

The resultant conflict and the reformation placed in motion nationalism, and afterward, the citizens of Western Europe defined themselves not solely as Christians but as the citizens of their respective nations. It is in this reformist view of citizenship that Western Europeans re-evaluated the social contract. The social contract which is defined as an implicit agreement among members of a society to cooperate for social benefits or protection. At its most atomistic level, the "social contract" traces man from his/her most natural state to his/her most socially organized state; from a lone resident of nature to a "citizen" of society. Jean-Jacques Rousseau described a transformation from "animal like" creatures of appetite and instinct to citizens bound by justice and self-prescribed law. John Hobbes' views of the social contract were grounded by self-interest; pre-organized man was motivated by lone self-interest, which he/she learned to constrain for the furtherance of self-interest.

Now let us place the three historical events into context, specifically, in England. Agricultural advancement led by the previously mentioned factors increased food production. Agricultural advancements lessened the labor requirements for crop production, and restrictions on crop pricing and internal regional exportation were loosened. Inefficient producers suffered, as producers who embraced the technological advancement were rewarded by the state. The state passed enclosure acts during the eighteenth century, which allowed for the private purchase of formally classified common areas, and the consolidation of smaller farms into larger specialized farms.

The enclosures acts were significant for another reason; it relaxed the feudal aristocratic stranglehold on land ownership. A rising mercantile class embraced technology and socioeconomic changes to profit from their exchanges of agricultural products. They were no longer constrained by state price controls and openly utilized the open loan interest system to borrow and lend funds to capitalize their mercantilist ventures. They were challenging an hereditarian hierarchal system to replace it with a surplus materially defined system. In France, the burgeoning capital rich merchants resided and conducted business in distinct boroughs, which became synonymous with the term bourgeoisie.

The loss of the commons increasingly made it difficult for peasants to survive solely on subsistence farming, and technological advancements pushed a large percentage of agricultural workers out of the vocation. The peasant connection to the land was lessoned; no longer were serfs as valuable to the landowner as the land. In simple economic terms, the peasants became abundant in a market, where once they were scarce. This led to massive dislocations, which witnessed thousands of formally land-attached peasants freed to move from small townships to larger towns and cities.

The Initial Western Dislocation

The dislocation of the feudal ties to the land are the first breaks in the communal nature of the social contract, and the first challenge to the communal ties of proximity. Polanyi (1944) described a *double movement*. A period of unheralded market expansion in which Western governments embraced the liberal creed and a *laisse fair* approach to land and former peasants. He described a *counter movement* or intervention in which labor demanded concessions, which at their core were appeals to reinstate communal safeguards, are vestiges of the previous sociopolitical order. Karl Marx described the period within the framework of class and predicted a proletarian reaction that similarly relied on the reinstatement of communal safeguards.

The nineteenth-century sociopolitical dislocation must be viewed within the context of geographic proximity and the reordering of the social contract. Feudalism relied on transactional interactions between citizens dictated by the legal norms of the Western social contract. Hobbes prescribed a moral tenet that dictated transactions between fellow "entitled" members of society, ".... morality is just a seat of rules for expediting the rational pursuit and coordination of our own interest without conflict with those other people who are doing the same thing" (Mills, 1997, p. 15). Hobbes description is of a moral code that dictates interactions between citizens that are codified by law and/or tradition.

The feudal system was maintained by religious obligations, but sociopolitical and economic dislocation disturbed and transformed the previous social orthodoxy. The binding nature of secular contracts became the binding glue of the contract. No longer were the obligations solely to provide services up the hierarchical social order. Contracts for services or goods crossed the once static social order that strictly guided interactions; labor was traded for compensation across the social order. Compensation tied to the ultimate system of production became the onus of the system.

Guaranteeing that transactional cost obligations were enforced were transferred solely from the ultimate threat of removal from the shared religious body or death. The failure to meet a contract obligation was enforced by the forfeiture of accumulated compensation or the removal of an individual from the social trading order, the market. The proximity of citizenship became dynamic with the enclosure of the commons and the migration to the urban. The communal ties of rural subsistence reordered to a wage contract system. The primal kinship and parish ties were disturbed, and with it a break in the previous communal sociopolitical contract.

Faux Citizenship the Racial and Feminist Contract

Charles Mills (1997) delineates a second aspect of the "social contract" that defined the strictures of the transaction cost binding only to members of the community of Western Europeans, the "racial contract." During feudalism, excommunication separated one from the community of the faith, and absent membership one was left to the whims of the faithful. The death of feudalism witnessed a re-ordering of excommunication; no longer was a breach of ecumenical law the maxim for exclusion. Birth outside of the community of the faithful became demarcated by race; "Race" gradually became the formal marker of this differentiated status, replacing the religious divide "whose disadvantage, after all, was that it could always be overcome through conversion" (Mills, 1997, p. 23).

The re-visitation of the social contract after 1648 must dually be examined within Mills' "racial contract" and the natural outgrowth of increasing nationalism and mercantilism. Mercantilism is a product of nationalism and is a system that encouraged the concept that government practice internationalism, sometimes defined as trade, to gain national wealth. It was a move away from the internal agricultural system as the sole economic basis of European economies. It was this mercantile competition between nation states; not monarchs, that initially was fostered by the plundered riches of South and North America. The tangible product of mercantilism was colonization, and it was colonization in the Americas, Africa, and Asia that cemented the death of Western European feudalism.

The increased international interactions by Western Europeans resulted in the introduction of newly demanded agricultural goods. These goods were grown in faraway newly colonized territories in the Americas, Africa, Asia, and the Caribbean. The populations of Europeans in these newly colonized territories were sparse regarding the increased demand of labor to produce the newly demanded agricultural products or to harvest raw natural resources. The answer to the labor shortage in the western hemisphere was slavery, a global industry of capturing, transporting, and marketing captured humans from the African continent. The answer to the labor shortage in Asia and Africa was the initialization of "Colonialism," a system of co-opting indigenous populations for the sole purpose of exploiting economic resources.

The juridical foundations of colonialism and slavery historically were codified to delineate the transaction costs for interactions between Europeans and non-Europeans. Slave codes in America, Indian laws in India, and colonial native acts formally codified the subordinate status of non-whites, and ostensibly "white privilege" for Europeans (Mills, 1997, p. 26). Interactions between Europeans and non-Europeans were played out through the above lenses of separate legally defined classes, thus giving privileged rights to some, and denying those rights to others based on skin color.

Conclusion

The African presence in America began at a historical period in which Western feudalism was witnessing its lasts gasps. Feudalism was grounded in an agrarian/rural social system and a pre-capitalist economic system. Mercantilism spurred by nationalism began to overtake feudalism as the dominant Western social system, just as colonization in the Americas began to tease Europeans with newly demanded agricultural goods. The African presence in the Americas was initially as labors to produce the demanded goods for European appetites.

The American social order was predicated on a continuation of agriculturally based feudalism, with the caveat of race, the racial contract. The racial contract exists because of its exclusionary nature. Simply, acceptance within the contract with full rights based on skin color overtly defines the basic contours of the contract. Conversely, exclusion from the contract, with no entitled protections, again reinforces the parameters of the social contract. Captive Africans were excluded from the social contract, and the basis of their exclusion was skin color. Feudalism does not exist outside the context of an agrarian system that ties labor to the land; however, emigrating Europeans were throwing away the yokes of hereditary defined ties to land. Yet riches were to be made by producing the new staples of European consumption: tobacco, indigo, and sugar. The solution was found by the creation of a new social order defined just as much by race as economic class.

Chapter 2

America & the Communal Contract

"I prefer to be true to myself, even at the hazard of incurring the ridicule of others, rather than to be false, and incur my own abhorrence. America is false to the past, false to the present, and solemnly binds herself to be false to the future. The thing worse than rebellion is the thing that causes rebellion."

Frederick Douglass

The United States exists within a duality of the social contract. It is constrained by the geographical nature of the social contract, but concurrently sociopolitical institutions developed that lessoned the scope of the constraint. Within the framework, the United States failed to develop a nationally sociopolitical response to industrialization, and relied on the local communal contract, "the union shop." Yet a system of government, federalism, with institutions engineered around proximity to citizens mitigates and provides an invisible efficiency to the American social contract. Dually, the United States is constrained by its locus to the "racial contract" that prevents the full incorporation of all its citizenry within the social contract and cements tribal static appeals for the seminal communal contract.

What Makes the United State Different?

In the preceding chapter, we discussed the genesis of feudalism, and its reliance on a shared religious tradition, Roman Catholicism. The United States began as an outgrowth of imperialism, as Western European colonies. The settler Western citizens rebelled against the extractive colonial system and formed an independent nation; however, the historical institutions that developed and grew were not dissimilar from imperial institutions. The Western colonizers incorporated the legal norms of the imperial powers, but their distance from the imperial powers allowed the growth of institutions that were free from feudalistic vestiges. According to Hartz (1955) and Fukuyama (2014, p. 136), "The United States was different...because it lacked the inherited feudal class structure of Europe."

For the newly nationalized nation and men of clear European heritage, an American embrace of "liberalism" became the basis of the newly minted social contract. Liberalism based on the enlightenment philosophy of freedom. Individualism is at the heart of liberal theory, which holds that given intellectual freedom, institutions will develop into "pareto optimizing" organizations. Samuel Beer (2006, p. 695) defines the premise, "According to liberal doctrine, the reason men should be free to govern themselves is that they can think for themselves." The American founders embraced the ideas of liberalism and individualism to craft a constitution based on cementing individual freedom.

The American revolutionists were not rejecting European citizenship, they were claiming that they were not receiving the privileges of citizenship and established an agrarian republic with landed elites at its helm. The mantra of the American revolution was "No taxation without representation." The mantra holds that men of European descent would not be held to the extractive process of colonization. For the most part, the American landed elite, held no aristocratic titles, but they inhabited a socioeconomic space on par with the European gentile class.

We must not forget that the measure of eighteenth-century wealth was land ownership. European exploration opened Western European markets to agricultural products from semi-tropical climates: rice, indigo, tobacco, sugar, and cotton. The Western European internal demand for the products spurred colonization. In the Americas, European settlers organized large agricultural farms, plantations, to produce the newly demanded agricultural crops. The control of land utilized to produce crops was the seminal means of building or sustaining wealth. An additional vocation developed around the land and crop production, which involved the logistical movement of crops from the American continent to the European. Merchants organized shipments and acted as wholesalers between producers, farmers, and shipping interest. Attorneys developed a burgeoning industry in which they ensured that the transactions between merchant, farmer, and shipper met legal requirements and that all parties were legally indemnified. If we list the signees of the American Declaration of Independence, there were seventeen plantation owners, eleven merchants, and twenty-one attorneys.[1]

The economic reality of the American revolutionists was closer to the agrarian system that preceded the industrial revolution, the imperial aristocracy, and the

---

[1] Additionally, there were four physicians, one minister, and one printer/scientist. The level of education of the men also made them unique in their colonial societies, but the level of wealth was unmatched with America's wealthiest families included (Phillips 2002, p.5): "...a Massachusetts Hancock, a New York Livingston, a Carroll of Maryland, a Lee of Virginia, and a South Carolina Rutledge."

burgeoning European mercantilist class. Most of the signees of the American Declaration of Independence were directly involved in the production of demanded agricultural products, the plantation owners and farmers, or were serving in auxiliary roles in the exportation of products, merchants and lawyers. For the imperial aristocrat or the landed gentry, colonial extraction and rents were the chief means of sustaining or building wealth.

The British institutionalized representation for the landed gentry, who were separate from the peerage class within the bicameral legislative body of parliament with its House of Commons and Lords.[2] Many of the American gentry were gifted land, plantations, which were equally their sources of wealth: William Byrd received a 1,200-acre crown grant in 1673; the great grandfather of Robert E. Lee, Robert "King" Carter was granted over 300,000 acres of land in what is now Virginia in the early eighteenth century; and a second descendent, Carter Braxton signed the Declaration of Independence.[3] The American colonist formed regional and local representative institutions, but there was no representation in the imperial institutions, and appointed colonial governors served at the pleasure and direction of the monarch. There were no colonial gentry members of the House of Commons. Thus, when excessive extractive acts were passed (The Sugar Act, 1764, and the Stamp Act, 1765), the burgeoning American landowning elite rebelled. The signers of the Declaration of Independence were declaring that they were being treated outside the bounds of the social contract, which as members of the gentry, they were entitled. The following quote from the Declaration of Independence speaks to the signees' contention that the British crown had relegated them outside the bounds of the social contract: "He [King George] has refused to pass other Laws for the accommodation of large districts of people, unless those people would relinquish the right of Representation in the Legislature, a right inestimable to them and formidable to tyrants only."

The American landed gentry did not establish a new state that rejected the imperial state. They created a similar state, with the landed elite at its head. The newly cemented constitution did not grant suffrage to all able-bodied citizens. It initially distinguished citizenship or suffrage for landowners, white male landowners. The seminal act of citizenship in any democracy is the right to vote (Dahl, 2003). By limiting the core act of democratic citizenship, the writers

---

[2] Peerage refers to the hereditary titled aristocracy, whereas the gentry were members were commoners.

[3] The legal granting of land to American settlers was via the headright system. It was a system in which the Virginia Company of London and the Plymouth Company granted land for settlement in North America and consisted of 50 to 100-acre plots.

of the American constitution were legally defining complete membership within the social contract for fellow landowners.

The newly cemented American constitution further concentrated institutional power to the landed elite with its inception of the legislative branch and the method of electing/choosing both senators and the chief executive. The "New Jersey Plan" was a compromise in which the writers of the United States constitution mitigated the potential electoral power of more populous states over less populous states. The legislative body was organized into a bicameral body with proportionally allocated representation within the House of Representatives and allocated two Senators for each state.

Theoretically, the Senate would act as a bulwark against the majority-dominated House of Representatives. James Madison (Hamilton et al., 2005) defined the institutionalized majoritarian constraints interwoven into the constitution within *Federalist No.10*. Madison argued that the size and plurality of the country would prevent the rise of *factions* and force compromise. He wrote, "The influence of factious leaders may kindle a flame within their particular States but will be unable to spread a general conflagration through the other states." Madison was articulating the existence of proximity within the social contract, while dually arguing that institutions like the senate would act to mitigate the passions of the majority or the communal nature of the social contract.

Table 2.1: 1774 Per Capita Income by region.

	All Wealth	In 2020 Dollars	Non-Human Wealth	In 2020 Dollars
South	£93.00	$14,953.92	£36.40	$5,852.93
Middle	£46.00	$7,396.56	£40.20	$6,463.95
New England	£38.00	$6,110.20	£36.40	$5,852.93
Britain (1688, G. King)			£55.00	$8,843.72
Britain (1770, A Young)			£135.00	$21,707.31

Source: Per Capita Wealth by Region, *The Statistical History of the United States,* p. 1175; British and other data from Alice Hanson-Jones, *Wealth of Nation to Be,* pp. 301-302.

The institutions did act as a bulwark against the threat of majority rule, but also as a means of sustaining the status quo. A status quo that afforded the

American landed gentry the exclusive reins of power. A further examination requires an exploration of pre and post-American inequality. Viewing *Table 2.1*, one will observe that in 1774 American per capita income trailed that of Britain, and that regionally the South was the richest and New England the poorest (Hanson-Jones, 1984). The North was the most populous region, but the poorest, if we subtract human wealth (slavery). We will further observe that per capita income between the North (New England) and the South evens out at approximately £36.40. This is important because it unmasks the true nature of American pre-revolutionary wealth.

The true nature of pre and post-revolutionary wealth was the owning and managing of large plantations maintained by captive labor. The population of white southerners compared to the population of white northerners was sparse. This meant that non-forced free labor in the American South was scarce, and as *Table 2.1* reflects, southern wealth was correlated to slavery. Additionally, the percentage of 1810 slaves working in agriculture outpaced that of whites, with 16 percent of slaves working in rural agriculture as opposed to 15.3 percent of whites (U.S. Census Bureau, 2015). This correlates with the agricultural basis of the republic and its feudalistic nature.

The colonial exportation of tobacco grew steadily during the seventeenth century and became a main export to London, with colonial exports of tobacco rising steadily from the 1630s to 1700. Tobacco thrives in a dry arid climate, and Virginia, with its relatively dry climate, became the center of colonial Tobacco production. Tobacco did not require large work gangs for its production, but labor was scarce. Large and small planters initially relied on the indentured servitude system to meet the labor demands, but the sparsely populated colonies could not meet the labor demand and forced African slave labor steadily became the answer.

The utilization of forced slave labor is and was antithetical to the liberalist ideology of the American founders, but it was perfectly in-line with a feudalistic system based on land ownership. Mills (1997) identifies a bifurcated Western social contract, with identifiable exclusions based on skin color, the racial contract. The "racial contract," within the context of American slavery, intersects with the "communal contract," as it is based on proximity and attaching a class of people to land, with an elite class of landowners, the American landed gentry, at its apex. The 1860 Census highlights that for white southerners, only 23 percent owned slaves, that only 6.6 percent owned 10-99 slaves, and that 0.1 percent owned 100 or more slaves (U.S. Census Bureau, 1860). This is important within the context of the need for large work gangs at large agricultural plantations, and it highlights the rank inequality of the system.

As earlier noted, the climate within the area of the Virginia colony was ideal for producing tobacco, and the exportation of tobacco to England plateaued at the end of the seventeenth century, but a newly demanded crop would spur the demand for increased labor, clearly define the land-centered "racial" social contract and push white class inequality. That newly demanded crop was cotton; the European demand for cotton spurred the codification of the American racial contract.

The Virginia House of Burgesses in 1661 enacted legislation that read, "…. providing that certain Negros would serve for life (Jordan, 1961, p. 245)." The reading is significant when viewed in the context of Elizabeth Key. Key was the daughter of a white Virginian, a member of the House of Burgesses, and an African mother. Key's father acknowledged his paternity, and Key was baptized as a member of the Church of England. Before her father's death, he arranged her guardianship under a legal document, an indenture. The guardian returned to England before the expiration of the indenture and transferred or sold the indenture to a second man, who held Key beyond the legal term of the indenture agreement. In 1658, Key sued for freedom for herself and her infant son arguing that based on their English ancestry, her status as a Christian, and the record of her indenture entitled her to freedom. Key won the case, but given her legal victory and the increased demand for labor, the Virginia House Burgesses passed a law in 1661 with the significant principle of *partus*.

Partus sequitur ventrem, often abbreviated to *partus* is a rejection of British common law for earlier Roman law. It rejected paternalism and assigned the legal status of African descent to the mother. Thus, the sons and daughters of African American women would follow the legal status of their mothers, not their fathers unlike all Englishmen. The rhetorical conflict between Massachusetts Judges John Saffin and Samuel Sewall in 1700-01 signified the change in the perception and treatment of African captives in America. Judge Samuel Sewall produced his pamphlet a mere eighty-one years after the arrival of the first African captives to Jamestown, but it signified the change in the status of African Americans. Africans were no longer to be held in temporary servitude but were to be held in perpetual bondage; and the rationale for the bondage was eerily similar to the rationales of feudalism. In 1701, Judge Saffin wrote,

> [God]…who hath Ordained different degrees and orders of men, some to be High and Honorable, some to be Low and Despicable; some to be Monarchs, Kings, Princes and Governors, Masters and Commanders, others to be Subjects, and to be Commanded; Servants of sundry sorts and degrees, bound to obey; yea, some to be born Slaves, and so remain during their lives…

Judge Saffin's words mirror Mills' conception of the "racial contract" with Saffin arguing that transaction with Africans was outside the norms to be assigned to Europeans, and in essence, the African captives would become America's serfs with key distinctions: African captives did not share the same skin color, shared history, and, in the beginning, religion as their European captors.

The elite nature and agricultural grounding of the American system was based on the economic reality of cotton. In the modern world, we have forgotten the once scarcity of cotton. The fibrous plant was once only grown in northern Africa and India, the process of spinning the fibrous boll into linen strands was a guarded process, and, as such, cotton was the cloth of the elite. Additionally, we take for granted the comfort of cotton compared to wool. Cotton is light and breathable for summer and winter wear, it is easily dyed, easily laundered, and nonperishable in transport. During the eighteenth century, the English gained the cotton processing techniques from colonial India, and with the burgeoning of coal-powered industrialized looms, cotton cloth became the most demanded internationally traded product in the world.

The 1790 price of one pound of cotton was $.25 lb., which correlates to $7 in 2020 dollars. The 1790 price of cotton correlates to the luxury status of the crop, which was produced in northern Africa and India. Cotton requires a semi-tropical or tropical climate, which eliminates most of Western Europe as producers, but the North American continent, specifically, regions in what is now the southern United States, provided an ideal climate for the growing of cotton. In 1790, those regions had not formally become part of the republic, and the regions were collectively referred to as the Georgia Territory. During the beginning of the eighteenth century, the Georgia Territory was opened to settlement, and ripe for large plantations encaging captive Africans in work gangs for the cultivation of the cash crop, cotton.

It was cotton cultivation and the large commercial farms manned by forced African labor that spurred the burgeoning nineteenth-century American economy. The eighteenth-century plantation system established the model for American agricultural production and the exportation of the products via the conduits of northern seaports. American cities had their impetus as trading and embarkation areas, and in America's earliest history, the rural areas sprung as appendages to the embarkation areas of Philadelphia, New York, and Boston. The rural areas provided the substance required to maintain the urban (Judd and Swanstrom, 2006). These embarkation areas continued as conduits of both export and import in nineteenth-century America and were sustained by the exportation of southern agricultural goods, cotton.

The southern agrarian system was a product of the communal social contract. A minority of large landowners owned and operated massive southern plantations.

Plantations that attached captive Africans to the land as unpaid hereditarian laborer. A system that mirrored Western feudalism, with the caveat that the captives, serfs, were clearly identifiable by their skin color (Smith, 2017). The large commercial agricultural farms were the nineteenth-century economic engines of American economic growth. By the mid-eighteenth century, raw cotton constituted 61 percent of American exports (Beckert, 2014). In 1850, America produced a majority of the 1.2 billion pounds of worldwide cotton, which can be viewed in *Table 2.2*. America's economic advantage was tied to three factors: boundless land, free labor, and available credit (Beckert, 2014).

Table 2.2: 1850s Selected Cotton Consumption by nation.

1850s Selected Cotton Consumption		
Nation	**Consumed Cotton**	**Percent Imported from America**
	Millions (lbs.)	
Great Britain	800	77%
France	192	90%
Zollverein	115	
Russia	102	92%

Source: Beckert, Sven. 2014. *Empire of Cotton.* New York, Alfred A. Knopf.

Simultaneously, cotton became the impetus of industrialization. The eighteenth-century invention, the steam engine, became the mover of large English industrial looms. The English steam-powered looms became the urban centers of employment for once land-attached peasants dislocated by the *Enclosure* and *Poor* laws. The processing of raw cotton became an increasingly industrialized process located in large cities. In America, the production of raw cotton was the economic engine, but large urban areas in the Northeast were following the industrial examples of Britain and France. The Jeffersonian and Madison ideal of the agrarian republican soon fell into odds with industrialization.

Unique to the American constitution was the embedded context of the document for the continuation of a faux agrarian republic tied to the slavery, a distrust of centralized bank, and the proximity of government to the citizenry. The Three Fifths Compromise, the Electoral College, the non-popular election of senators, the distrust of a liberal stalwart, a central bank, and the power-sharing system, federalism, engineered into the government ensured a system that would tie governance to the local level and empower a feudalistic slave system. The initial compromise of the newly formed American constitution was the Bill of Rights, the first ten amendments to the American constitution, but, just as significant, was the "Three Fifths Compromise," which allowed for apportionment purposes alone, the less populous South to count captured African slaves as 3/5ᵗʰ inhabitants. The compromise ensured that the South receive unequaled representation in the lower legislative body of the American government.

Equally as important is Article Two of the United States constitution. Within Article Two, the Electoral College was established. The Electoral College and the initial requirement that senators be selected by state legislatures further cemented power within the hands of the landed elite.[4] James Madison, in *Federalist Ten*, argued that the Electoral College is a stalwart against the passions of "faction." Madison defined faction, "...as groups of citizens who have a common interest in some proposal that would either violate the rights of other citizens or would harm the nation as whole." In theory, the Electoral College, acts to tamper the passions of "faction," with the establishment of electors, chosen by state legislations, who would act soberly to the counter the potentially negative choices of an impassioned plebiscite. Alexander Hamilton gave furtherance to the argument within the *Federalist Papers*, when he writes, [The Constitution is designed to ensure] "...that the office of the President will never fall to the lot of any man who is not in an eminent degree endowed with the requisite qualifications." The ultimate choice of who holds the Office of the Presidency does not solely lie with the people, who initially were landed white males. Alexander Hamilton's description of the Electoral College mirrors that of his fellow founders, but his seminal belief in a central tenet (central banking) of the liberal creed, put him at odds with the proponents of the agrarian republic.

In 1791, Alexander Hamilton, as America's first Treasury Secretary, established America's first central bank to eliminate revolutionary debt and provide a mechanism of financing the American government. The establishment of the bank immediately fell into odds with the proponents of the agrarian republic. Jefferson, a large plantation owner, who was in a constant state of debt to foreign banks, argued that the national bank jeopardized the individual and that banks were the purview of the states. Thus, for Jefferson, the national bank violated the powers enumerated to the national government. Jefferson and his ally James Madison proposed that banking allowed speculation, and that speculation resulted in wealth outside the norms of work. It is a plausible argument but

---

[4] The 17ᵗʰ Amendment, which was not ratified until April 8ᵗʰ, 1913, set the direct election of United States senators.

must be taken within the context of land ownership. Jefferson and Madison's source of wealth and status was land ownership. Banking challenged the status-quo, and a communal agrarian economy. Yet, the country and the world were slowly falling in line with capitalism and the liberal creed, both require banking and national central banks. In 1811, then President Jefferson allowed the charter for the first national bank to expire, but less than a decade later, 1816, a second bank was organized, as a result of both governmental and private demands. The issue of the agrarian republic persisted with another southern plantation owner, President Andrew Jackson, dissolving the Second Bank of America in 1836.

Jefferson and Madison utilized the threat the bank posed to the individual as an organizing principle of their political ideology and America's first political party. The argument lies within the context of American government organization, which is defined as federalism. Federalism, a term that is not included within the American constitution but is at the heart of government power allocation to the central and state governments. Jefferson and Madison argued that banking was not an enumerated power granted to the central government; therefore, it is an implied power reserved for states. The argument plays out within the proximity of government to citizenry and the communal contract, yet it was proffered as egalitarian when, in fact, it was a veiled challenge to an institution that jeopardized the status quo.

Conclusion

The chapter highlights what makes America different within the scope of the dynamic social contract. The history of American institutions and the dominance of the racial contract are the seminal factors, but, in 1791, the inception of federalism delineated institutions and their proximity to citizens. Federalism is defined as a compound mode of government that combines a central government with regional (state) governments in a single system. It is this system that has defined the American social contract within the geography proximity.

Chapter 3

American Federalism

"Since taking office, one of my first priorities has been to repair the machinery of government and…to make government more effective as well as more efficient."

President Richard Nixon, 1969 Television Address on Federalism

"Government is not the solution to our problems. Government is the problem."

President Ronald Reagan, First Inaugural Address, 1981

"We are going to rethink the entire structure of American society, and the entire structure of American government.… This is a real revolution."

Speaker of the House Newt Gingrich, 1995

The above quotes were from remarks given by American political leaders. The remarks both summarized their governing philosophies and were preludes to the launching of "reforms." The word reform was left in quotation purposely to highlight the ambiguity of their maxims. The word reform within the context of policy equates that there was policy failure that required correction. Timothy Conlan (1998) asserts that the initiatives were a response to the failures of the centralizing "Creative Federalism" of President Lyndon Johnson and the stalwarts of the New Deal. Their goal was advanced decentralization or devolution. It is within the context of devolution, not policy failure that is the key.[1] Devolution is defined as the transfer or delegation of power to a lower level, especially by central government to local

---

[1] The idea cannot be confused, with the burdensome liberal state described by Theodore Lowi (1969). Lowi argued that pluralism, interest groups, captured the state, within the captured state, administrative agencies grew. Clientelist interest groups that solely pushed self-interested policy prescriptions.

or regional administration. Devolution is a synonym for the communal social contract and has its genesis in the Jeffersonian notion of the agrarian republic.

The American government is constructed within the framework of federalism. Federalism designed within the bounds of proximity to government. A proximity that mirrors the contours of the communal social contract. The production of governmental services is decentralized, and citizens often encounter their interactions for service within the communal or local context of the social contract. The American central government institutions can be described as quiet. A quietness that is often mistaken for nonexistence, and that when inefficient is overly generalized by the proponents of the communal contract.

The quietness of the American central government is borne out by the words of the proponents of the American constitution. In *Federalist 10*, James Madison writes under the collective pseudonym of *Publius* and gives definition to both the quietness and nature of the American central government:[2]

> The other point of difference [between a republic and democracy], is the greater number of citizens and extent of territory which may be brought within the compass of republican than of democratic government; and it is this circumstance principally which renders factious combinations less to be dreaded in the former than in the latter.

Madison makes three important points about the new government and nation. He gives definition to Republic and defines its differences from a democracy. He defines representative democracy (Republic). And he argues that the expansive territorial nature of the country dictates the need of representative democracy and quiets the factious nature of local differences.

Madison's definition of democracy was historically unique. It was historically unique within the context of the term and practice. In the Western world, democracy is derived from Greece. The Greek city-states, Athens, Sparta, Corinth, and Thebes. The actual word, democracy, originates from two shorter words: *"demos"* meaning whole citizen living within a particular city-state and *"kratos"* meaning power. We can loosely put the words into meaning: "the citizens rule." The citizen rule was distinctly located within the Greek city-state of Athens, and was what Madison described as a "direct" democracy, for ancient Athenian male citizens, over the age of twenty. It was the duty of the males to directly take part or be chosen by lottery, *sortition,* as officials.

---

[2] Publius Valerius Poplicola was one of four Roman aristocrats who led the overthrow of the monarchy, and the establishment of the Roman Republic.

Madison combined the Greek democracy, with the Roman republic. Republic, as a system of government, begins within the city of Rome in 509 BCE, when the Roman people overthrew their monarch and replaced the monarchy, with elected magistrates, tribunes. The Latin definition of republic is a form of government in which "power is held by the people and their elected representatives." It is a misnomer that the Roman Senate was comprised of elected officials. It was not. The magistrates were the elected representatives of the people, and the Roman senate, served an advisory function. Initially, only patricians, participated in the process; however, about sixty-years after the overthrow of the Roman monarchy, plebeians formed an assembly called the "Concilium" which was able to elect ten tribunes, or representatives, annually, but suffrage was held solely by male citizens. Madison combined the terms democracy with republic to argue that the new government was a combination of the two, a representative democracy.

The third contour of the new system of government was based in space, geography. Madison was writing before the great western expansion that united the country between the Pacific and the Atlantic oceans, but the size of the original thirteen colonies dwarfed that of eighteenth-century England. In the modern United States, eleven states are larger than eighteenth-century England, and, in total land mass, the United States is slightly less in mass than Europe. Madison argued that the land mass of the new country nullified attempts to build a centralized direct democracy. In short, the geographic space precluded the organization of a direct democracy. Additionally, Madison argued that expansive geography would tamper local factious behavior from growing beyond local boundaries.

It is Madison's contention that geographic distance tampers the growth of local factious behavior that is at the heart of the quietness of the American central government. Madison was describing factions within the realm of political parties, which he initially viewed as negative. America exists within the framework of Westphalian sovereignty. American institutions exercise authority within its borders and are efficient. If a serious crime is committed within the territorial United States, including secluded expanses of rugged territory (northern Alaska) local, state, or federal law enforcement will have a presence, not in days but hours. Often, the law enforcement presence will be of state or local authority. It is the bounds of this local response in which the quietness of the American central government exists and is born out of the words of the United States Constitution:

> "The powers not delegated to the United States by the Constitution, nor prohibited by it to the states, are reserved to the states respectively, or to the people."

Tenth Amendment, U.S. Constitution

In other words, the states have all powers not granted to the federal government. It is within this shared context of government in which the powers of the central government are "*enumerated*" or defined. The system relies heavily on local and state governments and has resulted in the expansion of governments at the local level, with over 88,000 distinct governments existing within the American system. In the following section, we will examine the growth of the American population within the context of federalism, which manifests in a locally focused decentralized government interactions that mirror the communal social contract.

Rural verse Urban

The United States Constitution was ratified in 1789, there were thirteen states geographically straddling the Atlantic coastline. The population centers of the newly organized nation were the east coast core cities: Boston, New York, Philadelphia, Baltimore, and Charleston. Each was organized near or on the intersections of natural ports or accessible tributary rivers. The cities were the locus of international trade facilitated by the embarkation or importation of goods via natural harbors. In 1789, none of the core cites had reached a population of 10,000. The nation only totaled 3.9 million people, the 2019 population of the state of Nevada. The core cites were bordered to their east by the expansiveness of the Atlantic Ocean and to the west by the unexplored frontier. Like all cities, the country or rural area serves as a conduit of agricultural stuffs that are required to feed and sustain an urban populace. America was no different, the founding and organizing of the cities preceded the organization of the rural areas needed for their maintenance.

The 1790 geographic outlays of the United States population give context to the notion of the rural republic. The cities must be viewed in economic context, the cities were the mechanical conduits of agricultural production. In 1790, the full-throttle dynamism of the industrial revolution had not yet shown its marks. The mainstay American exports were agricultural: tobacco, cotton, furs, skins, salt meat, flaxseed, rice, tar, turpentine, and pitch. The rural population outpaced the urban, as the producers of the agricultural mainstays of exportation and the sustenance providers of the urban core. The 1790 urban population was five percent of the total United States population. The rural verse urban population proportions give context to the Jeffersonian and Madison context of the rural republic.

The context of the rural republic would last into the nineteenth century, but the cities as the mainstays of finance and trade would overtake the rural in a century. In 1817, the New York State legislature authorized the financing of the construction of a 364-mile waterway to connect Lake Erie to the Hudson

River. The project was completed in 1825, and in the words of Dennis Judd and Todd Swanstrom (2006, p. 21),

> ...it became possible to ship huge volumes of agricultural and extractive goods from the continental interior through the Great Lakes to Buffalo down the canal, and on to the port at New York, where they could be distributed along the eastern seaboard, used in factories, or shipped to Europe.

The canal shortened the shipping time that was required to ship goods via the Ohio, Missouri, and Mississippi rivers to the New Orleans ports. The canal served as a direct pathway from the rural agricultural heartland to the financial center of the nation. It vaulted New York to the primary center of American trade, finance, and population, by 1860, with 62 percent of American trade flowing through its ports (Judd and Swanstrom, 2006).

The success of the Erie canal spurred other states to invest in canals and by 1840, state-subsidized and operated canals traversed over 3,000 miles of American waterways, but an even more efficient mode of transport was on the horizon (Judd and Swanstrom, 2006). On July 4, 1828, thirteen miles of railroad tracks were laid from the Baltimore harbor. The initial construction spurred a boom in railroad construction and regional rivalry. Following 1828 were rail lines laid in 1832 by the South Carolina Canal and Railroad Company, which constituted the longest rail line in the world at 136 miles. Early lines were completed in 1834 in the eastern seaboard, the Columbia Railroad of Pennsylvania and the Boston and Providence lines in 1835.

Rail lines and canals were infrastructure projects that made both travel and the transportation of goods more efficient. A second aspect of both canals and railroads was that the intersection of lines spurred initial localized population and economic growth. Chicago and Kansas City became the locus of railway transport because of their central locations, and Chicago's location as both a port of egress and a railway hub. In 1859, Chicago railway lines connected it to Pittsburg and eleven other trunk lines, and only ten years later, in 1869, rail lines connected from the west coast and the east coast in Utah to traverse America. From the half-century mark of 1850 to 1900, the network of railway tracks expanded from 9,021 miles of track to 258,784.[3]

---

[3] U.S. Department of Commerce, *Historical Statistics of the United States, Colonial Times to 1970*, pt.2, pp. 728, 731.

The possibility of economic growth spurred communities to subsidize railway lines, with both land and capital, but the specter of federalism was ever-present. The initial attempt to provide a central government-supported transportation network was proposed in 1808, by then-Treasury Secretary Albert Gallatin, with his plan for a federal system of turnpikes and harbor improvements. Regional rivalries, which James Madison famously declared would tamp down factious behavior simmered in congress over support of the plan, which ultimately failed to gain congressional approval. In 1830, twenty-two-years later, congress passed a turnpike bill, that succumbed to the veto of then-President Andrew Jackson, whose administration viewed transportation within the scope of the agrarian republic, as a state matter not a federal responsibility (Judd and Swanstrom, 2006).

States took up the mantra of subsidizing railway expansion within the guise of economic development. The impetus that railway lines would spur economic and community growth led investment in railway construction at the community level. It must be remembered that in the mid-nineteenth century, the initial stock offering IPO was not a relevant means of raising capital for embryonic privately held companies. The enterprises relied on government subsidies initially from the states but later from local communities. The boom to build spurred ever-increasing competition and investment from local communities, with the ultimate hope that a successful rail line would lead to the externalities of economic and population growth.

By 1861, state and local communities had provided a substantial percentage of the capital to private railway enterprises, with 25 to 30 percent of all direct investment in railroad building supplied by state and local governments, with the following breakdown of spending: cities $300 million in direct subsidies; states $229 million in direct subsidies; and the federal government $65 million in direct subsidies (Judd and Swanstrom, 2006).[4] Let us put the scope of the subsidies into context by utilizing inflation and converting $300 million in 1861 to its present-day dollar value, 2021, which equals $9 trillion. The entire united states federal budget in 1861 was $82 million, which converts to $2.5 trillion in 2021 dollars. The overall government investment in railway building from its conception, roughly from 1828 to 1861 dwarfed any other public investment in a private enterprise in the history of the United States.

The cities being the biggest player in public financing of railway building, began utilizing the then-novel instrument of municipal bonds to subsidize

---

[4] In addition, the federal government and states offered generous land grants to the railway companies, which the companies converted to cash by selling to settlers.

railway investment. The capital raised from the issuance of bonds was then utilized to purchase stock in fledgling railway enterprises, build terminal facilities, and clear rights of way. In the 1850s, the strategy witnessed the successes of Denver and Kansas City, which utilized the bond process to both grow into successful regional transportation hubs, but the overelevation of railway investment, unscrupulous railway enterprises, and regional rivalry quickly turned to bust.

An earlier economic panic, the Panic of 1837, which witnessed the failure of scores of railway and canal enterprises led to substantial losses of taxpayer-funded and private investment. Several state legislatures responded by 1840 with legislation that included prohibitions preventing public financing of private enterprises. The bubble burst during the economic panic of 1873, railway lines crisscrossed the country, and municipality after municipality had gambled on the hope of investment with the issuance of millions of dollars in municipal bonds. In 1873, one-fifth of municipal debt was tied to railroad bond defaults, $100 million to $150 million of municipal debt.[5]

State legislators composed of representatives from both rural and urban communities but dominated by rural populations began to reject responsibility for the cascading debt that flowed from defaulting municipal railway bonds. The rural urban divide was beginning to draw lines within the realm of fiscal policy. Rural residents, who were geographically removed from the urban areas, did not feel that their tax dollars should be utilized to bailout the urban areas. As a result, many state legislatures passed legislation that restricted local debt and the aid that could be given to private corporations by municipalities (Judd and Swanstrom, 2006).

The growth and expansion of the American rail system expanded the industrial output of the growing nation, but it also highlighted the indifference of governance that permeated through the American system. An indifference that was buttressed by space. The American system of federalism fostered an indifference toward urban policy, and at the state level, the rural urban divide was apparent. "More than anything else, rural legislators wanted to keep urban politicians and the constituencies that supported them from intruding into their domain (Judd and Swanstrom, 2006, p. 41)."

The rural verse urban divide is not unique to America, and political coalitions involving agriculture, industry, and labor have been historically fractious. Peter Gourevitch (1986) highlights the parameters of the economic

---

[5] A.M. Hillhouse, *Municipal Bonds: A Century of Experience* (Upper Saddle River, N.J.: Prentice Hall, 1936), p. 39.

collapse of 1873, and the political coalitions that developed from the crisis that witnessed agricultural and industrial coalitions not only in America but Germany. The coalitions not only crossed methods of production but the geographic space of production, which further highlights the dynamic nature of the social contract. The industrial aspect will be further explored in the proceeding chapter but must be included as the exploration moves toward highlighting the legal basis of the dynamic social contract, which is easily highlighted by America's *de facto* racist history.

States' Rights—The United States Constitution to Jim Crow

The United States is a Constitutional Democracy, and America's initial constitution, the Articles of Confederation, was a loose confederation of independent states, with a weak central government. The initial document highlighted a geographic embedded conflict that has historically swelled and ebbed as America faced socioeconomic strife. The context of the conflict is often vocalized within the contours of American federalism, but the maxim has traditionally centered on the power of the central government verses the policy preferences of individual states. A geographically distant central government verses the policies preferences of the local and state governments.

The American war for independence ended in 1783, and the American victors, whose mantra was, "...no taxation without representation," instituted a new constitutional government within a weak confederation of thirteen semiautonomous states. The rationale was linear, former American colonists rebelled against what they believed was an onerous central government, the British. The specific policy that was onerous was taxation. The American colonist rebelled against the extractive practices of colonialism and formed a government without the power of taxation. Within the Articles of Confederation, the individual states had the sole authority to levy taxes. The central government was required to request funds from individual states, and outside the bonds of domestic policy, individual states could negotiate foreign treaties. The reality of the Articles of Confederation was that the new nation was composed of thirteen sovereign states.

In 1787, the thirteen semiautonomous states of the United States were embroiled in disputes over territory, revolutionary war pensions, taxation, and trade. It would not be a stretch to believe that many Americans, including prominent citizens, believed that the newly independent nation was near the brink of collapse. Fifty-five of these prominent citizens met in secret during the summer of 1787 in Philadelphia, Pennsylvania to craft a second American constitution. The resulting document strengthened the central government and introduced the concept of federalism, but it did not end embedded geographic conflict; it set a standard of compromise.

As discussed in the previous chapter, the New Jersey plan established a bicameral legislature, but central to regional compromise was the "Three-Fifths Compromise," which allowed enslaved captives in the South to be counted as three-fifths citizens during the census, for apportionment purposes. The compromise enabled the less populace southern states to seat a disproportionate delegation within the House of Representatives, and coupled with each state seating two senators, the compromise enabled the southern states to wield political power disproportionate to its population.

The power of the central government is *enumerated* within the American constitution, but historically the United States has witnessed an incremental adoption of federal law at the state level. The statutory supremacy of the central government in the American system is established within the American constitution, *Article VI, Paragraph 2* of the United States State's Constitution, which establishes that the federal constitution, and federal law generally, take precedence over state laws and state constitutions. The Supreme Court of the United States further codified federal supremacy, with the seminal nineteenth-century decisions in *Marbury v. Madison, 5. U.S. 137* (1803) and *McCulloch v. Maryland 17 U.S. 316* (1819)[6]. which dually established judicial review, with the federal judiciary and federal law at its apex. However, within the realm of civil rights and civil liberties, the United States Bill of Rights singerly applied to the federal government until the ratification of the 14th Amendment (1868) and the fifteenth Amendment (1870) of the U.S. Constitution in a process known as incorporation, which leads us to the enumeration of the uniquely American concept of *states' rights*.

The concept of state's rights can be traced to the Articles of Confederation, but the ideological birth of the concept lies with the origins of the agrarian republic, Thomas Jefferson and James Madison. In 1798, the United States government was controlled by the Federalist, with John Adams holding the office of presidency and the Federalist holding key majorities within the legislature. The federal government responded to a diplomatic dispute, the *"X,Y,Z Affair,"* with the newly minted Republic of France. In 1796, the French reacting to the 1794 *Jay Treaty* with Britain, which sought a maritime resolution with America and Britain following the American revolution, responded with an order allowing for the seizure of American merchant vessels.

---

[6] The additional nineteenth Century cases of *Gibbons v. Ogden 22 U.S. 1* (1824); *Worcester v. Georgia 31 U.S. 515* (1832); *Ableman v. Booth 62 U.S. 506* (1858); and *In re Neagle 135 U.S. 1* (1890) the U.S. Supreme Court reaffirmed the supremacy of the federal government.

In 1797, an American diplomatic delegation was dispatched to France to resolve the maritime dispute, however, the delegates were refused an audience with the French foreign Minister, the Marquis de Talleyrand, but were approached by three French intermediaries: Nicholas Hubbard (later W,) Jean Hottinguer (X), Pierre Bellamy (Y), and Lucian Hauteval (Z). The intermediaries demanded the following: that the United States provide France with a low-interest loan, assume and pay American merchant claims against the French, and lastly pay a substantial bribe to Talleyrand.

The American delegation sent dispatches detailing the French demands back to the American president, John Adams. After receiving the dispatches, President Adams prepared for war, and pro-war Federalists pushed Congress to support him. American opposition leaders were suspicious of Adams' motives and demanded that he publicly release the diplomatic correspondence describing the negotiations in France. Adams, knowing its contents, obliged them and released the correspondence, but replaced the names of the French intermediaries, with the letters W, X, Y, and Z. The resultant dispute led to the undeclared "Quasi War" with France.

The pro-war Congressional Federalist passed the onerous Alien and Sedition Acts in 1798. The four laws raised the residency requirements for citizenship from five to fourteen years, authorized the President to deport aliens and permitted their arrest, imprisonment, and deportation during wartime. Jefferson and Madison, the opposition leaders, secretly responded to the laws by writing the Kentucky and Virginia Resolutions, which provide the ideological foundation of state's rights and nullification. The resolutions called for state legislatures to nullify "unconstitutional" federal laws. Jefferson argued that the United States, the federal union, is a voluntary association, and that if the central government enacts legislature it determines to be onerous that each state has the right to nullify the law, as Jefferson wrote in the Kentucky Resolution:

> Resolved, that the several States composing the United States of America, are not united on the principle of unlimited submission to their general government; but that by compact under the style and title of a Constitution for the United States and of amendments thereto, they constituted a general government for special purposes, delegated to that government certain definite powers, reserving each State to itself, the residuary mass of right to their own self-government; and that whensoever the general government assumes undelegated powers, its acts are unauthoritative, void, and of no force: That to this compact each State acceded as a State, and is an integral party, its co-States forming, as to itself, the other party....each party has an equal

right to judge for itself, as well of infractions as of the mode and measure of redress.

The ideological seeds of nullification reared again during the 1830s over economic policy. If we separate America of the nineteenth century into two regions, North and South, we will observe the same economic model that preceded the American revolution. The South's primary economic tool was agriculture, but by the 1830s, the industrial revolution was well cemented in the American North with burgeoning industries. The South was heavily dependent on international trade or trade with the North for manufactured goods, but in contrast, the burgeoning northern manufacturing industries saw international trade in manufactured goods as competition. In 1828, the American Congress passed protective tariffs that benefited northern producers.

In 1832, the state of South Carolina responded to the tariff with legislation, *South Carolina' Nullification Ordinance*. The ordinance followed the nullification logic laid out by Jefferson and Madison thirty years earlier. The language of the ordinance, passed by a state convention on November 24th, 1832, declared that both the tariffs of 1828 and 1832 were null and void within the state borders of South Carolina. The action cemented a crisis that brought the nation to the brink of violence, with then President Andrew Jackson dispatching naval warships to South Carolina's coast and threatening to send federal troops to the state to enforce the tariffs. An exert from President Jackson's military authorization follows, "…[that] our social compact in express terms declares, that the laws of the United States, its Constitution, and treaties made under it, are the supreme law of the land" and for greater caution adds, "that the judges in every State shall be bound thereby, anything in the Constitution or laws of any State to the contrary notwithstanding."

The economic dispute ended peacefully, but the ideology of nullification persisted and enveloped the definition of American citizenship within the context of slavery. In the previous chapter, we discussed the racial contract, and how it was defined within the context of slavery. Specifically, that American captives of African descent were excluded from the privileges of the social contract based entirely on skin color. The nullification conflict, that one can argue began with the American constitution's tacit legalization of slavery and definition of citizenship, resulted in actual attempts of nullification, the Civil War.

The economic reality of pre-Civil War America was two economic systems which were witnessed by the tariff crisis of the 1830s: a burgeoning industrial economy in the North and a feudalistic agrarian economy in the South. Compromise cemented political equilibrium. For most of the nineteenth century, the two regions witnessed historical political compromise that was witnessed by the *1820 Missouri Compromise* and the *Kansas Nebraska Act*, which both appeased the southern agrarians by reinforcing political equilibrium, but, in many respects, the conflict between the American North and South was a prelude to the twentieth-century conflict between the Wilsonian liberalists and the Leninist, in which modes of production defined allegiances. The southerners embraced the "old-world" communal contract, and the northerners embraced the dynamism of the liberalized social contract.

The southerners argued within the context of the racial contract and utilized the nullification arguments presented by Jefferson and Madison. The context of the proslavery argument devolved into property but were manifestations of the racial contract. Slaves were not Europeans, and, by extension, were excluded from the social contract. The exclusion from the social contract allowed for slaves to be treated or classified as the "others." In the case of American slavery, as chattel or property. The manifestation of the argument carried that the central government did not have the right, within the social contract, to exclude its privileged members from their property, people of African descent held in captive servitude.

In 1857, the position was endorsed by the Supreme Court, with its ruling in *Dred Scott v. Sanford: 60 U.S. 393* (1857). The case involved Dred Scott, an enslaved man who was transported to free territories and back to the enslaved territory. Scott argued that his residency in free territory amounted to tacit emancipation. The case reached the American Supreme Court, which was led by southerner and Chief Justice Roger Taney. Chief Justice Taney and his supporters on the court ruled against Scott, but also, they rejected the century-long political compromise between the American North and South. The Taney court ruled that all Americans of African descent, either enslaved or free, were non-citizens, and excluded from the privileges of citizenship. Additionally, the court established that slavery crossed both enslaved and free territory, with its judgement requiring mandatory enforcement of the fugitive slave laws.

The ruling effectively accelerated the path to nullification in the American South. The context of the American Civil War was state's rights, the rights of individuals within secessionist states to hold other men in bondage. This is clear by the reading of state session statements, and an excerpt from Georgia's Secessionist Statement follows:

> The people of Georgia having dissolved their political connection with the Government of the United States of America, present to their confederates and the world the causes which have led to the separation. For the last ten years we have had numerous and serious causes of complaint against our non-slave-holding confederate States

with reference to the subject of African slavery. They have endeavored to weaken our security, to disturb our domestic peace and tranquility, and persistently refused to comply with their express constitutional obligations to us in reference to that property, and by the use of their power in the Federal Government have striven to deprive us of an equal enjoyment of the common Territories of the Republic. This hostile policy of our confederates has been pursued with every circumstance of aggravation which could arouse the passions and excite the hatred of our people, and has placed the two sections of the Union for many years past in the condition of virtual civil war. Our people, still attached to the Union from habit and national traditions, and averse to change, hoped that time, reason, and argument would bring, if not redress, at least exemption from further insults, injuries, and dangers. Recent events have fully dissipated all such hopes and demonstrated the necessity of separation.

The conclusion of the American Civil War did not witness the death of the state's rights ideology within the context of American politics. In the preceding sections of the chapter, we discussed the incorporation of the American Bill of Rights. One of the primary criticisms of the American constitution made by its opposition, the Anti-Federalist, was its lack of an enumeration of civil rights and liberties. Prior to its ratification, the first ten amendments to the United States constitution were added, the Bill of Rights. However, within the context of the American system of federalism, the enumerated individual rights only applied to the Federal government. At the conclusion of the Civil War, the Thirteenth, Fourteenth, and Fifteenth Amendments were added to the American constitution. The Thirteenth Amendment ended American slavery, and the Fourteenth and Fifteenth Amendments incorporated the Bill of Rights along all the tiers of American government; however, the application of incorporation was temporary.

The conclusion of the Civil War witnessed the close of American feudalism, but soon after the conclusion of the Reconstruction era, the American racial contract was retooled within the scope of a skin color-based caste. The feudalistic system was replaced with caste, which retooled the distinction of chattel and replaced it within the scope of a skin color defined inhuman standing. The enumeration of the system was codified by *de facto* statutes and *de jure* practices. The system segregation, began with a rejection of the expansive nature of the Thirteenth and Fourteenth Amendments within the context of American federalism.

A dispute over state regulation, specifically, within the New Orleans seaports grew to be the seminal case that rejected incorporation and allowed citizenship status to be defined at the local and state level. In 1873, the Supreme Court delivered a decision regarding a dispute between local butchers and the State of Louisiana. The Louisiana state government instituted sanitary regulations regarding the butchering of livestock within the New Orleans ports. Several butchers objected to the rules and argued that the privileges or immunities clause of the 14th Amendment was violated by the state of Louisiana, with the regulations and filed suit, *The Slaughter-House Cases, 83, U.S. 36* (1873). The Supreme Court ruled that the Privileges or Immunities Clause of the Fourteenth Amendment to the U.S. Constitution only protects the legal rights that are associated with federal United States' citizenship, not those that pertain to state citizenship. The ruling gave *carte blanche* to the redefining of citizenship for Americans of color, who would no longer be protected at the local and state level by the protections of the Fourteenth Amendment.[7]

The racial social contract was codified in 1896, with *Plessy v. Ferguson, 163 U.S. 537,* (1896). The case set in motion the establishment of the American race-based caste system, segregation, by establishing the Separate but Equal doctrine. The case involved a New Orleans man, Homer Plessy, who in 1892 refused to give up his seat to white passengers on a New Orleans trolley train. Plessy was arrested and convicted. Plessy argued that his rights were violated and appealed the case to the United States Supreme Court. The Supreme Court ruled against Plessy and held that if segregated facilities were equal in quality, Americans of color could be served separately from the white population. The case formally allowed for the *de facto* establishment of the American caste system under the auspicious of "Jim Crow." Local segregation laws were enacted throughout the country, but most intensely in the American South: laws that required separate public schools, separate public accommodations in restaurants, separate hospitals, separate cemeteries, separate public restrooms, separate water fountains, and prevented inter-racial marriages.[8] The codified segregation laws

---

[7] The Supreme Court further rejected incorporation with *United States v. Cruikshank* (1876). The case arose after African Americans were massacred after protesting election results, the Colfax Massacre. The Supreme Court held that the 14th Amendment did not apply to the 1st or 2nd Amendment to state governments in respect to their own citizens, only to acts of the federal government.

[8] In the *Civil Rights Cases* (1883), which preceded *Plessy v. Ferguson,* the Supreme Court again rejected incorporation by striking down the Civil Rights Act of 1875, a statute that prohibited racial discrimination in public accommodation. It again held that the Equal Protection Clause applied only to acts done by states, not to those done by private individuals, and as the Civil Rights Act of 1875 applied to private establishments, the Court said, it exceeded congressional enforcement power under Section 5 of the 14th Amendment.

were followed by *de jure* practices and cemented by violent terrorism upon people, white or black, that rejected the system.

The Progressive Age

Outside the bounds of racial politics, the state's rights ideology temporarily tamped down at the beginning of the twentieth century. The contours of the racial caste system were set, and Americans began to grabble with the vestiges of the communal contract constructed within the architecture of the federalist system. American historians refer to this period as the *Progressive Age*. It was a period in which the patronage system was replaced by civil service, and "reform" motivated policy makers began to deconstruct empowered urban political machines with reformed city government structures. The reality of the period fits more into the context of the dynamic social contract. Political and economic elites were challenged by the communal nature of machine politics, whose practitioners, immigrants, relied on the communal ties of language, national origin, and religion to build powerful political coalitions that not only asserted power at the local level but at the state and federal levels. The response of the elites was retrenchment against the communal contract and an embrace of the imagined national community, as described by Benedict Anderson (1983).

In the preceding chapter, we discussed how James Madison described the United States Senate as a bulwark against the House of Representatives, with its local "factious" demands, which we can argue can be motivated by the context of the communal contract. The original selection of senators was removed from the communal context, and the American constitution required that senators be selected by state legislatures. In 1913, the United States constitution was amended, with the Seventeenth Amendment, which allowed for the popular election of the United States. Senators. Additionally, 1913 witnessed the passage of the Sixteenth Amendment, which imposed a federal income tax. Both changes to the United States constitution limited the control of the states over the central government. Both changes to the United States. Constitution were responses to the communal contract, but the most salient changes occurred in the population centers, the large cities.

A flood of European immigrants restructured urban politics during the last decades of the nineteenth century and the first decades of the twentieth century. The United States expansive territory, abundance of natural resources, and demand for labor witnessed a flood of European immigration during the last decades of the nineteenth century and the first two decades of the twentieth century. The urban centers were bustling with new factories, which demanded unskilled laborers. A flood of European immigrants inundated the urban centers to feed the demand, and America's central cities bustled with ethnic-centered neighborhoods (See *Table 3.1* for illustration). Concurrently, a shift in agricultural technology increased crop efficiency and freed millions of Americans from rural agriculture.

Table 3.1: U.S. Immigration from 1820-1919 by national origin.

	1820-1829	1830-1839	1840-1849	1850-1859	1860-1869	1870-1879	1880-1889	1890-1899	1900-1909	1910-1919
Total in millions	0.1	0.5	1.4	2.7	2.1	2.7	5.2	3.7	8.2	6.3
Percentage Total:	40.20%	31.70%	46%	36.90%	24.40%	15.40%	12.80%	11.00%	4.20%	2.60%
Ireland	4.5	23.2	27	34.8	35.2	27.4	27.5	15.7	4	2.7
Germany	19.5	13.8	15.3	13.5	14.9	21.1	21.1	8.9	5.7	5.8
United Kingdom	0.2	0.4	0.9	0.9	5.5	7.6	7.6	10.5	5.9	3.8
Scandinavia	1.8	2.2	2.4	2.2	4.9	11.8	11.8	0.1	1.5	11.2
Canada					0.2	1.3	1.3	12.2	18.3	17.4
Russia					0.2	2.2	2.2	14.5	24.4	18.2
Austria-Hungary					0.5	1.7	1.7	16.3	23.5	19.4
Italy										

Source: U.S. Department of Commerce Bureau of the Census, Historical Statistics of the United States. Colonial Times to 19701: and Current Population Reports, Series P-23, Ancestry and Language in the United States; November 1979.

The context of the social contract for the first waves of European immigration between 1820 and 1919 followed the logic of the communal nature of the social contract and advanced from kinship, ethnicity, region, faith, and nationalism. A context of citizenship, defined as a form of exchange among privileged members (Riesenberg, 1992). Exclusion from the population of privileged members excluded one from even exchange. The first waves of immigrants, the Irish, were not defined members. The second wave of immigrants, the Germans, were defined members because of their socioeconomic status, and the third wave, the Italians, were like the Irish and excluded.

The first wave of European immigrants were the Irish fleeing the famine of the 1840s potato blight. The Irish were peasant subsistence farmers that relied on the hearty potato and other vegetables for survival. The 1840's potato blight swept Europe but witnessed its most disastrous effects within

Ireland, which can be witnessed by a five-year period between 1845-1850 when a quarter of the Irish population succumbed to starvation. Thousands of the survivors embarked from Liverpool ports to America. During the same period, a German civil war pushed thousands of educated and middle-class Germans to flee their homeland for America. The immigrants disproportionally settled in American cities, with over half of the 1870 population of America's twenty largest cities identifying as foreign-born or second-generation citizens (Judd and Swantstrom, 2006).

Table 3.2: American Illiteracy Rates 1870-1950.

Year	Total	White	Native	Foreign Born	Black
1870	20	11.5			79.9
1880	17	9.4	8.7	12	70
1890	13.3	7.7	6.2	13.1	56.8
1900	10.7	6.2	4.6	12.9	44.5
1910	7.7	5	3	12.7	30.5
1920	6	4	2	13.1	23
1930	4.3	3	1.6	10.8	16.4
1940	2.9	2	1.1	9	11.5
1947	2.7	1.8			11
1950	3.2				

Source: U.S. Department of Commerce Bureau of the Census, Historical Statistics of the United States. Colonial Times to 19701: and Current Population Reports, Series P-23, Ancestry and Language in the United States; November 1979.

The newly arrived Irish/Catholic American immigrants encountered the hostility of out-group discrimination. In 1900, only thirteen percent of the United States population identified as Catholic, which meant that much of the U.S. population were Protestant anglophiles, which is illustrated in *Table 3.2*. The Irish and Italian immigrants were Catholic, non-English speakers. The Irish were low-skill rural peasants. These factors placed the Irish, and later the Italians, outside the bounds of the American social contract. The exclusion from the social contract made the Irish and the Italians a target for discrimination. Because of their poverty, religion, and peasant origins, they became etched in the public mind as dangerous, alcoholic, criminal, and dirty. Anti-Catholic and anti-Irish riots broke out on a regular basis. Irish churches, taverns, and neighborhoods were attacked by mobs whipped up by a rhetoric that spoke of "an invasion of venomous reptiles..., long-haired, wild-eyed, bad-smelling, atheistic, reckless foreign wretches" (Judd and Swantstrom, 2006, p. 34). The wealthy and middle-class German immigrants social class status and education provided a shield against the discrimination that was faced by the Irish and Italians.

A social order developed in which class status defined the contours of the nineteenth and early twentieth-century America. The established "Protestant" Yankee was positioned at the top of the social order, with the socioeconomic power to hire and fire. A pecking order developed, with the Irish, and later the Italians, near the bottom, only above the African American. The contours of the social system played out within the geographic constraints of the social contract.

The geographic nature of the nineteenth and twentieth-century immigration reinforced the proximity aspects of the communal contract. Most immigrants settled in the most undesirable urban locales near waterfronts and factories. Unscrupulous landlords shepherded immigrants into crammed apartments and converted warehouses. During the decades of the 1840s, tenement housing developed in New York City, crammed apartments crowded with multi-families in tiny unventilated units.

Italian and Irish neighborhoods were the context of the densely packed neighborhoods. The inhabitants spoke the same language, practiced the same faith, and shared the same cultural traditions as their neighbors. It was this communal setting that enabled the rise of the communal-centered urban-based political machines, which we define as: a political group in which a single leader or a small group command the support of a corps of supporters, who receive patronage (benefits) for their efforts.[9]

The geographic concentration of immigrants into cities and the mass suffrage of white males created the perfect storm for the rise of urban machines. Prior to the 1820s, most mayors were selected by state governors or city councils, but in 1822 St. Louis and Boston revised city charters to allow for the popular election of mayors. Additionally, the property ownership requirement was removed as a voter eligibility requirement, which enabled native-born and naturalized white men the right to vote in mass, and that a key component of machine politics is voter mobilization. The increased suffrage of white male citizens incentivized office seekers to mobilize as many voters as possible within America's winner take all system.

Most United States cities are subdivided into political wards, and wards are composed of geographically contiguous neighborhoods. At the end of the nineteenth century and the beginning of the twentieth century, the large city

---

[9] The closed network of immigrant neighborhoods was one of three factors that led to the development of urban based political machines. The two key factors were the immergence of a mass electorate and industrialization (Bridges, 1984, p. 8).

neighborhoods were concentrated ethnically homogenous enclaves. First and second-generation immigrants resided in densely populated neighborhoods with fellow immigrants; Irish immigrants were the close neighbors of other Irish immigrants, and Italian immigrants were the close neighbors of other Italian immigrants. The densely packed ethnically homogenous neighborhoods were the perfect locales for the rise of political machines.

Political machines were historically organized with the machine boss at the top of the hierarchy and the ward captain at the bottom, see *Figure 3.1* for illustration. The ward captain's chief responsibility was the mobilization of the voters within his ward, and to accomplish this act, the ward captain was expected to be intimately connected to residents that resided within his ward. In the ethnically homogenous neighborhoods, in which residents shared a common language, a common faith, and common traditions this was not difficult, and the element of socioeconomic exclusion cemented by wider discriminatory practices created closed network connections that reinforced collective or communal ties (Feldmeyer, 2018). Within the system, above the ward captain was the alderman, who reported to the machine boss, often the mayor.

Figure 3.1: Political Machine Hierarchy.

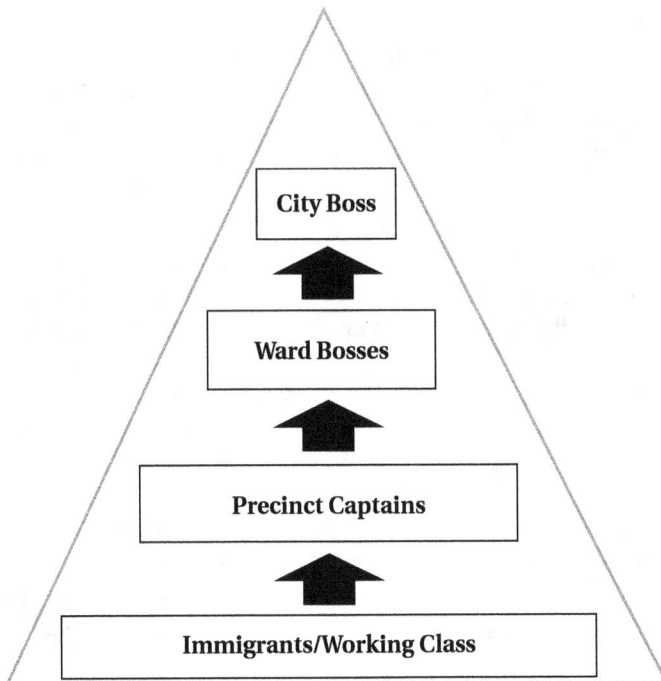

A simple one-word definition of the system is that it is transactional. The machine boss's objective is being elected and/or securing the election of allies. To win election, office-seekers need to win more votes than their opponents. To win more votes, office seekers need to mobilize more voters. The machine incentivizes their voters by promising and/or ensuring once in power that supporters will be rewarded via patronage, city jobs. The system worked perfectly in large, ethnically concentrated cities: New York, Philadelphia, Chicago, and Kansas City. The electoral footprint of the large cities within their states translated to not only local political power but to control of state legislatures and federally elected offices. The communal nature of machine politics is obvious, but the American response fits into the context of the dynamic social contract.

The response to the ethnically empowering nature of the machine politics was the Progressive Movement. A movement which emphasized reform, but simultaneously limited the power of machines and, by extension, ethnic voters. Chief among the reforms, was the establishment of civil service rules and reformed city governments. The primary tool of the machine was patronage. Establishing civil service guidelines within urban governments eliminated patronage, and negatively impacted ethnic job seekers. Civil service is based on a merit system, which requires that job applicants display their aptitude via pre-employment exams. This disadvantaged foreign-born applicants whose illiteracy rates were three times higher than the national average, for illustration see *Table 3.3*, (U.S. Department of Commerce, 2021). The removal of patronage eliminated the primary tool utilized by machine systems to reward members. Additionally, reform city government structures, with weak mayor designs weakened the chief office of the machine boss.

The guise of the Reform Era was clothed in a national appeal to the imagined community, but ultimately it was aimed at restricting the power of "non-members" from the privileges of the social contract. The dynamics of the racial contract deluded the non-member status for both Irish and Italian Americans, but the long-term dynamics of the American assimilation of the Irish and the Italians was the context of the racial contract. Generational assimilation predicated upon skin color dissipated the out-group status of the Irish and Italians. Sociologists Robert Park and Ernest Burgess (1925) developed the "Classical American Assimilation" model in which they chronicled the upward mobility of Chicago's immigrant groups, and their generational movement from dense ethnically homogenous neighborhoods located in the urban center to generational social class movements outward to outer ring ethnically heterogenous communities. Italian and Irish American's membership in the American social contract was solidified by the mid-twentieth century, but for other American immigrants, the racial contract was in full effect.

Table 3.3: U.S. Illiteracy rates from 1870 to 1979, including foreign born.

Year	Total	Foreign-born
1870	20	-
1800	17	12
1890	13.3	13.1
1900	10.7	12.9
1910	7.7	12.7
1920	6	13.1
1930	4.3	10.8
1940	2.9	9
1947	2.7	-
1950	3.2	-
1952	2.5	-
1959	2.2	-
1969	1	-
1979	0.6	-

Source: U.S. Department of Commerce, Bureau of the Census, Historical Statistics of the United States, Colonial Times to 1970; and Current Population Reports, Series P-23, Ancestry and Language in the United States: November 1979.

The racial contract and immigration played out within the context of Asian immigration to the United States. In 1882, Congress passed the *Chinese Exclusion Act* and *Alien Contract Labor laws* in 1885 and 1887. The Chinese Exclusion Act closed off immigration from China, and the Alien Contract laws were aimed at low-skilled Asian immigrants. Congress continued with the *Immigration Act of 1917* that halted all immigration from Asian countries.[10] It

---

[10] The Immigration Act of 1924: limited the number of immigrants allowed into the United States yearly through nationality quotas. Under the quota system, the United States issued immigration visas to 2 percent of the total number of people of each nationality in the United States at the 1890 census. The law favored immigration from Northern and Western European countries. Great Britain, Ireland and Germany accounted for 70 percent of all available visas. Immigration from Southern, Central and

was not until seven years after the conclusion of World War II that the anti-Asian immigration laws were rescinded in 1952, with the *McCarran-Walter Act* that ended the exclusion of Asian immigrants to the United States.

States' Rights—The Great Depression to Insurrection

The context of American federalism and the social contract were expanded during the Great Depression and the conclusion of World War II. The New Deal Coalition comprised of northern labor, southern "Dixiecrats," and Western agriculture emerged from the economic decline, with an embryonic socioeconomic safety net.[11] Social policies centered on redistributive policy designed to lessen the ills of economic decline emerged but could not ultimately withstand the dynamics and the nature of the social contract. A primary fission in the coalition was the "States Rights" mantra, with its outright appeals to the racial contract.

The refusal of southern Democrats to coexist in a political coalition with African Americans was evident by the 1948 third-party presidential segregationist candidacy of Strom Thurmond, on the States Rights Democratic Party ticket. Southern Democrats were angered by President Truman's *Executive Order 9981*, which was issued on July 26, 1948, that integrated the armed forces. They were further angered by Minneapolis Mayor Hubert Humphrey's speech during the 1948 Democratic convention, in which he advocated the inclusion of an anti-segregationist plank in the party's electoral platform. Thirty-five delegates from Alabama and Mississippi walked out the convention and later formed the States Rights Democratic Party.

The 1948 presidential election resulted in a stunning victory for incumbent Harry S. Truman, but the beginning of a racial realignment of the electorate was evidenced by Strom Thurmond receiving 1,169,021 popular votes and 39 electoral votes. The previously solid Democratic states of Louisiana, Mississippi, Alabama, and South Carolina were all carried by Thurmond (See *Map 3.1*). Historically, with the ending of Reconstruction, the southern states were primarily a one-political-party region (Key, 1949). The Republican Party was virtually non-existent in the South, and African Americans were

---

Eastern Europe was limited. The Act completely excluded immigrants from Asia, aside from the Philippines, then an American colony.

[11] *Wickard v. Filburn*, 317 U.S. 111 (1942) allowed the federal government to enforce the Agricultural Adjustment Act, providing subsidies to farmers for limiting their crop yields, the court proclaimed agriculture affected interstate commerce and came under the jurisdiction of the Commerce Clause even when a farmer grew his crops not to be sold, but for his own private use.

systematically denied their right to vote. It signified that, unlike in the beginning of the twentieth century, that America's racial contract; specifically, concerning African Americans is dynamic.

Map 3.1: 1948 & 1968 Presidential Election Results

1948 & 1968 Presidential Election Results

Legend
- Strom Thurmond Won States
- Thomas Dewey Won States
- Harry Truman Won States

Legend
- Wallace Won States
- Humphrey Won States selection
- Nixon Won States

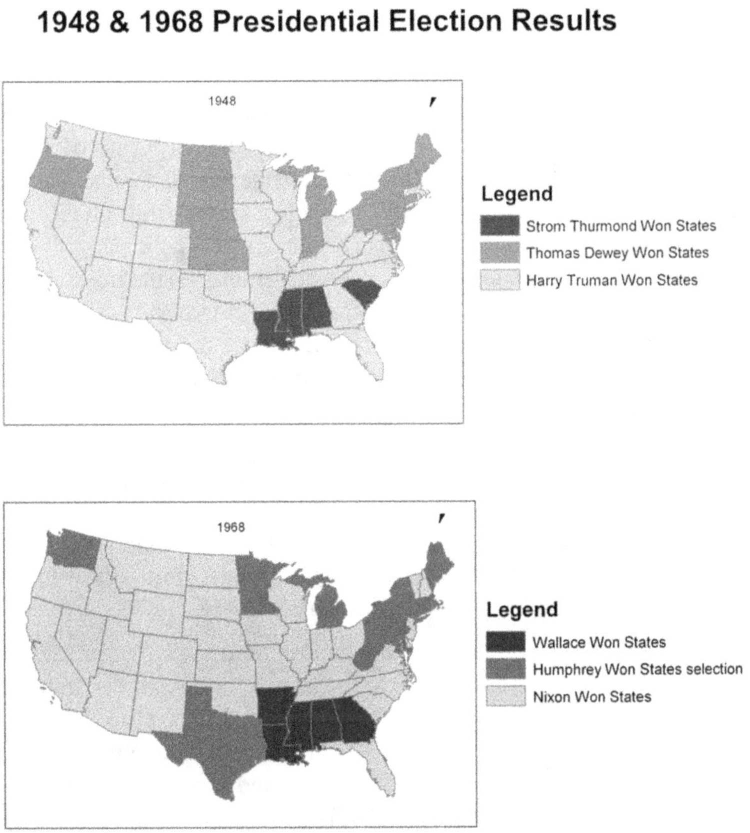

Strom Thurmond received 1 electoral vote from TN for the 1948 election

The 1964 and 1965 passages of the Civil Rights Act and the Voting Rights Acts reignited the issues of the racial contract. The Civil Rights Act and the Voting Rights Act coupled with the 1954 Supreme Court case of *Brown v. Board of Education of Topeka*, 347 U.S. 483 effectively overturned the legal structure of the American caste system but reignited the debate within the realm and scope of the earlier ideology of the agrarian republic. The earlier nineteenth-century question of African American citizenship resulted in the supreme court declaring in the *Dredd Scott v. Sandford* case that African Americans were not citizens, and after the Civil War, the courts ruled that the Fourteenth Amendment was unincorporated at the state level. Both rulings effectively eliminating or diminishing African American citizenship. The response to the legislature and court rulings from the 1950s and 60s ushered in a similar response, the rise of the conservative movement. A movement that can be defined within the context of the dynamic social contract, a retraction to an earlier social contract.

American conservatism is defined within the context of the status quo, or for our purposes, a static social contract. Barry Goldwater (1960) described the ideological concept of American conservatism as follows, "Conservatives take account of the *whole* man, as well as spiritual. While liberals tend to look only at the material side of man's nature, conservatism looks upon the enhancement of man's spiritual nature as the primary concern of political philosophy." Goldwater argues that the American conservative maxim is the maximization of individual freedom while maintaining the social order. William Buckley and John Passos (1959) argued that conservativism was the viable alternative to American progressives based on "...freedom, individuality, the sense of community, the sanctity of the family, the supremacy of the conscience, the spiritual view of life." We can break the American conservative movement down into four key tenets: a divine intent, as well as personal conscience, rules society; an attachment to an imagined American traditional community; a belief that a "civilized" society requires order and hierarchy; and that property and freedom are inseparably connected. We can add a fifth tenant, but only with a little "tongue and cheek," that society must change but slowly.

Historically, the American conservative movement began in the 1950s, and one can argue that it was a response to the fear of the spread of communism, but domestically it was a reaction to the Civil Rights Movement, which manifested within the conservative John Birch Society. The John Birch Society opposed the civil rights movement and claimed that the movement was overly influenced by communists with the goal of creating a "Soviet Negro Republic." The 1964 conservative Republican Presidential candidate Senator Barry Goldwater opposed the 1964 Civil Rights Act.[12] Additionally, conservative organizations, like the Federalist Society, founded in 1982 with the goal of influencing young attorneys and potential judges within a textualist and originalist interpretation of the United States Constitution, which they argue

---

[12] Senator Barry Goldwater was a member of the NAACP and active supporter of desegregation in Phoenix, Goldwater voted in favor of the Civil Rights Act of 1957 and the 24th Amendment to the U.S. Constitution.

is a rejection of the liberal Warren Court of the 1950s and 60s. The Warren court, which increasingly incorporated the elements of the Bill of Rights and the Fourteenth and Fifteenth amendments at the state and local level.

President Lyndon Johnson took office in 1963 following the assassination of President John F. Kennedy, and he initiated the last programs of the New Deal Coalition; programs which were opposed by the fledgling conservative movement. Unlike Roosevelt's New Deal, Johnson's Great Society was initiated during a period of economic growth. American gross national product averaged 8.5 for the two years 1964 to 1965, and family income over the same period rose by $1,000, but the national poverty rate was a staggering 22 percent (U.S. Census Bureau). As illustrated in *Figure 3.2*, poverty was concentrated by region in the South, with the state of Mississippi displaying an astronomical percentage of the poor, 55 percent. The poverty rate was not limited to poor African Americans. The 1959 white poverty rate was 17 percent, high but still below the 55 percent for African Americans (U.S. Census Bureau). On May 22nd, 1964, President Johnson presented his goals for the Great Society,

> We are going to assemble the best thought and broadest knowledge from all over the world to find these answers. I intend to establish working groups to prepare a series of conferences and meetings—on the cities, on natural beauty, on the quality of education, and on other emerging challenges. From these studies, we will begin to set our course toward the Great Society.

Figure 3.2: Percent poor by region, 1959.

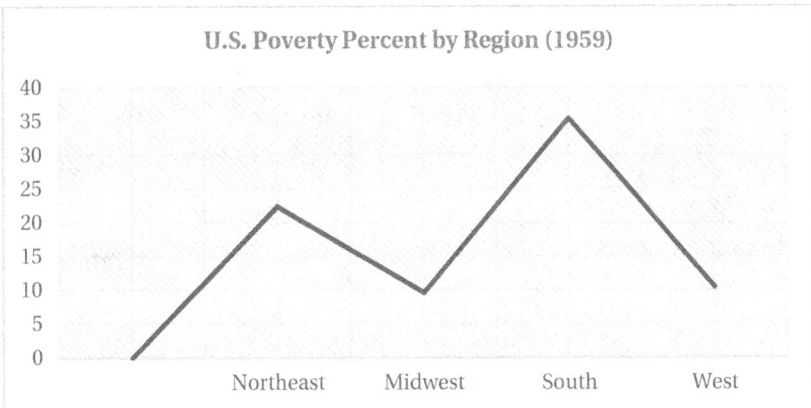

Source: Richard Morrill (2015). "50 Years of US Poverty: 1960 To 2010," *New Geography,* *https://www.newgeography.com/content/004852-50-years-us-poverty-1960-2010*, accessed 07/06/2021.

The Great Society programs were varied, but the stalwart initiative of the undertaking was the War on Poverty, which began with a one-billion-dollar congressional appropriation in 1964. From 1964 to 1966, a total of $3 billion was appropriated for the program. A laundry list of programs ranging from the Job Corps, whose purpose was to help disadvantaged youth obtain job skills to; the expansion of the Food Stamp programs; Headstart, and Community Action programs. The mainstay of the Great Society was direct funding of the initiatives by the federal government, and for conservatives this was a bridge too far. Conlan (1998) refers to this as centralizing "creative federalism."

Conservatives argue that the Great Society programs created an imbalance between the federal government and state governments, which disturbed their notions of federalism, and immediately judged that the programs were a failure. Their solution was retraction, devolution, and indirect funding of programs, in which the federal government simply provided the revenue and the states managed and defined program delivery or slashed funding to programs that conservatives believed were private goods. A chief example was Ronald Reagan's tenure as the conservative governor of California.

Ronald Reagan began his tenure as the conservative governor of California in 1967. While campaigning for governor, candidate Reagan lauded against what he described as the communist and left-wing disorder of California's state universities. Universities that offered free and reduced tuition to in-state students. Once in office, Governor Reagan enacted the following regarding higher education before declaring that the state, "...should not subsidize intellectual curiosity; ended free tuition for state college and university students; annually demanded 20 percent across-the-board cuts in higher education funding; repeatedly slashed construction funds for state campuses; and fired Clark Kerr, the highly respected president of the University of California" (Clabaugh, 2004; Minor 2008). Governor Reagan not only slashed California state spending on higher education but opposed increased spending on basic primary education. The burden of supporting local public schools was placed on local communities, which only recourse was to increase local property taxes.

The process of conservative devolution coincided with a sociopolitical response to the Civil Rights Movement. During the 1960s, both the federal courts and congress dismantled the statutory basis of racial caste. The mantra of the conservative movement was retraction or the maintaining of the American racial contract. National anxiety over the Vietnam War, the assassination of Dr. Martin Luther King Jr., and subsequent urban riots in Watts (1965), Washington D.C., and Detroit (1967) marked the period of the 1968 presidential election. "Nixon's claim to represent the 'silent majority' and 'the nonshouters and nondemonstrators' was an important symbolic statement to those who grew weary of the protests and demonstrations of the 1960s (Walton, 1997, p. 130)." Richard Nixon's words offered reassurances to white Americans, who viewed the violence of the urban riots negatively and who also viewed the results of the Civil Rights Era negatively. It was an appeal to white supporters of the racial contract who viewed the Civil Rights Era strides as a potential nullifying act to equalize and/or nullify the racial contract. The goal of the strategy was to attract southern conservative Democratic voters. The Nixon campaign utilized terms such as *law and order*, which played on white fears and stereotypes of African American community disorder.

> The implication of the strategy was that African American lawlessness would run rampant in white neighborhoods if Hubert Humphrey were elected president. It played on white economic fears by charging that "reverse discrimination was rampant in the United States workplace and confirmed to some that African American progress could come only at the expense of whites, an inference that was plumbed by the southern strategy" (Walton, 1997, p. 130).

It was within this context that President Ronald Reagan assumed the presidency and made the following statement during his 1981 inaugural address, "Government is not the solution to our problems, Government is the problem." The statement was an outright appeal to the conservative mantra of devolution, and within the narrow context of appeals to the racial contract. Ronald Reagan began his 1980 post-convention general campaign by speaking in Philadelphia, Mississippi, at the state fair. Philadelphia, Mississippi is very symbolic to the Civil Rights Movement. It was the location of the murder of three civil rights workers—James Chaney, Michael Schwerner, and Andrew Goodman. The men were murdered after being released by local police, who held them while they were in town investigating the burning of an African American church. When they were released in the middle of the night, they were kidnapped by angry racists and beaten to death. Their bodies were disposed in a roadside ditch.

During his speech, Reagan emphasized conservative themes, lauding the virtue and necessity of states' rights, promised to reduce the federal commitment to civil rights enforcement, and the Great Society economic programs that have benefited African Americans substantially. Not only were the words of the speech symbolic, but the location of the speech was ripe with symbolism (Lawson, 1991, p. 294). Philadelphia, Mississippi, is viewed negatively by supporters of the Civil Rights Movement, as it represents the worst of white supremacy and violence. Michael Fauntroy (2007, p. 132) writes that,

He played on many of the sentiments that had won the state for Barry Goldwater sixteen years earlier. It called attention to Reagan's social conservatism. The result of the controversy surrounding Reagan's appearance was that white conservatives found a measure of comfort in the fact that he was willing to incur the wrath of the civil rights establishment by showing that his racial views were similar to their own.

The American urban verse rural context was amplified by the Reagan era devolution policies centered within the declining federal support of urban areas. The core urban regions are often centers of industrial and financial production and are dually comprised of dense minority populations that are key supporters of the Democratic Party. M*aps 3.2, 3.3 and 3.4* illustrate the density of America's minority populations in the core urban centers, with African American dense populations in the South, Midwest, and Eastern seaboard cities. Hispanic dense populations can be observed in the Southwest, Florida and California coastal cities. The conservative Republicans were and are politically disincentivized to give fiscal support to the cities. The policies were aligned with earlier Progressive era policy that sought to diminish the political power of urban immigrants; the policy sought to alienate urban populations and to incentivize urban population flight.

Map 3.2: U.S. Population Density by County

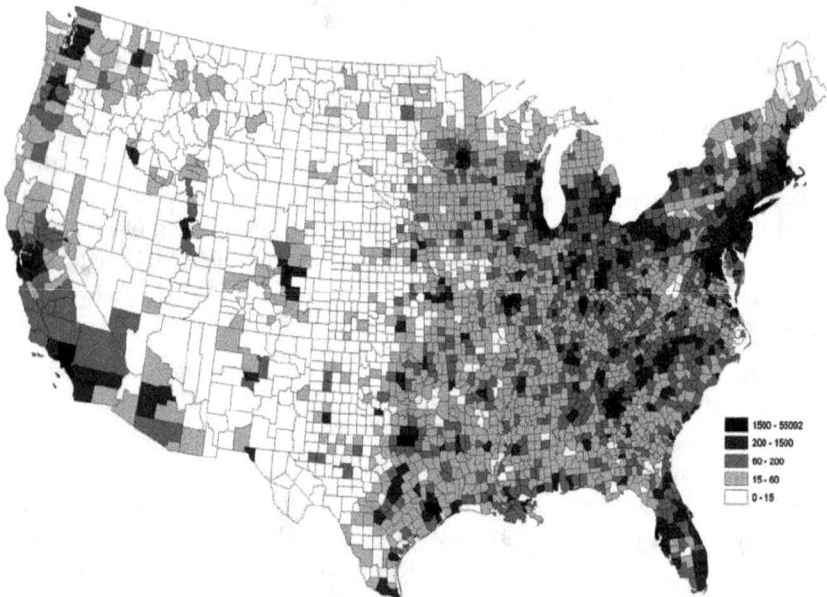

Source: U.S. Census Bureau (2021).

Map 3.3: African American Population percentages by county.

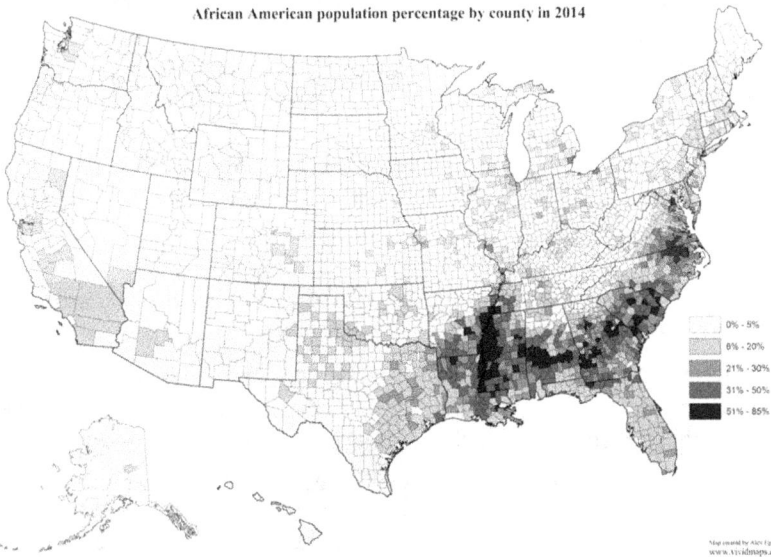

African American population percentage by county in 2014

Source: https://vividmaps.com/us-population-density/

Map 3.4: Hispanic Population percentages by county, 2014

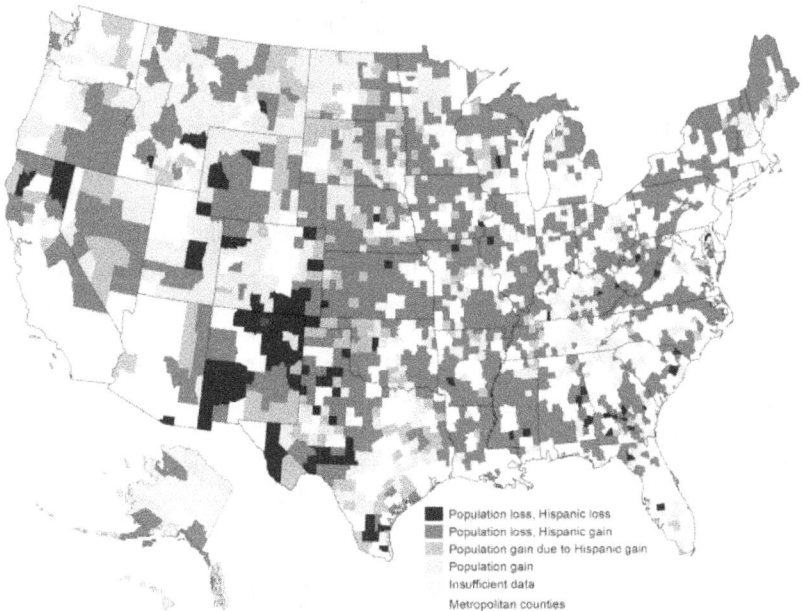

Source: https://vividmaps.com/us-population-density/

During the abbreviated presidential term of Gerald Ford and his predecessor Jimmy Carter, 1975 to 1980, federal aid to subordinate levels of government for community development block grants increased from $38 million to $3.9 billion but declined to $3.3 billion by 1987, during the administration of President Ronald Reagan (Stoesz, 1992, p. 153). From 1980 to 1986, the federal contribution for community services block grants decreased from $557 million to $354 million, and Housing and Urban Development program appropriations declined from $57 billion in 1978 to a low of $9 billion in 1989 (Stoesz, 1992, p. 153). Before President Reagan took office in 1980, federal aid accounted for 22 percent of large American cities' budgets, and by the end of his term, 1989, it was down to 6 percent (Lowenstein, 1995). The only program that survived the cuts was federal highway aid, which benefited suburban enclaves[13].

The unnuanced political appeals to racial contract continue to playout in American politics clothed in the ideology of conservatism. During the late 1990s, the Republican Party effectively lost an electoral footing in the most populous state, California, after pushing unpopular anti-immigrant legislature, but the appeals found footing during the 2016 presidential campaign. Then-candidate, Donald Trump, made salacious claims about Mexican immigrants and Mexican Americans. The unclothed appeals resonated with Republican voters and ensured an electoral victory. Trump was unable to reproduce the victory in 2020, due to high turnouts of minority voters in the central cities of Michigan, Pennsylvania, Georgia, and Arizona. Trump's response was to a twofold appeal directed first at the urban rural divide clothed in Progressive era unsubstantiated claims of central city voter fraud, and the second more nuanced appeal at the legitimacy of non-white voters.

The appeals resonated with many Republican conservative voters that adhered to claims of non-existent voter fraud. The process has culminated in an open insurrection on January 6, 2021, within the United States capital, and Republican state efforts similar to the Jim Crow era legislature to restrict voter access for minority voters. Similar to earlier pre-Civil Rights Era Supreme

---

[13] The Reagan administration continued the assault on the local or urban followed Significantly, President Reagan also took steps to increase state power over education at the expense of local school districts. Federal funds that had flowed directly to local districts were redirected to state government. Moreover, federal monies were provided to beef up education staffing at the state level. The result was to seriously erode the power of local school districts (Clabaugh, 2004). Spending on higher education was slashed by some 25 percent between 1980 and 1985. No federal program suffered deeper cuts than student aid. In raw dollar figures, cuts totaled $594 million in student assistance and $338 million in Pell grants (Fergus, 2014).

Court decisions, a conservative-dominated supreme court has failed to rule that the restrictive state-level laws are unconstitutional.

Conclusion

The context of American citizenship has historically been nestled within the framework of the social contract. It has been dynamic, restrictive, and is defined within the scope of the American federalist system. American geography has dictated conflict within the system, which is often dictated by the scope of the racial contract. The federalist system historically retracted at the beginning of the twentieth century, when the imagined American social contract was not abridged by race, with an established race-based caste system. The scope of the central government expanded, but as the statutory basis of the race-based sociopolitical order was eroded earlier claims of the imagined agrarian republic resurfaced under the guise of the state's rights mantra. The regressive appeals to an earlier communal contract have been clothed in the ideology of American conservatism, specifically, devolution. Devolution is a synonym for the communal social contract and has its genesis in the Jeffersonian notion of the agrarian republic. In the next chapter, we will examine the institutional genesis of labor within the American social contract, and we will observe a similar adherence to the communal contract.

Chapter 4

American Labor and the Constrained Double Movement

"It is essential that there should be organization of labor. Capital organizes and therefore labor must organize."

President Theodore Roosevelt

Douglas North (1990) described institutions as human constructs composed of informal or formal rules. The definition is important within an analysis of American industrialization. Pre-industrial American production existed within the last vestiges of feudalism, and feudalism set the context of early American production, the rules. The pre-revolutionary American economy was organized as an extractive enterprise to economically benefit the British empire. The American economy was organized to export agricultural goods, and ancillary production was geared to support agriculture. It was within this context that labor was organized in the newly independent nation. At the conclusion of the American war for independence, America was an agricultural society. Eastern cities were organized near natural harbors, locations ideal for the embarkation of agricultural goods demanded by Western Europeans.

The cities were conduits of agricultural production, and most of the population were either subsistence farmers, producers of exported agricultural goods, or the producers of food stuff demanded by the inhabitants of the Eastern cities. The 1790 census revealed that only five percent of the population of 3,929,000 (about twice the population of present-day New Mexico) resided in towns of 2,500 or more persons (U.S. Census Bureau, 2021). The image of late eighteenth-century American labor mirrored Jefferson and Madison's imagined rural republic. The small workshop apprentice model was the norm. Small producers manufactured on demand. The American society was organized around agriculture, maritime activities, fishing, and sparse workshop industries. American labor demands were tailored to its needs: primarily to satisfy the needs of farmers; secondly, to satisfy maritime trades; and finally, to satisfy both workshop industries and the skilled crafts.

Pre-industrial American cities mercantile locus was the water, rivers, and seaports. The center of urban production and residences, warehouses, docks, banks, taverns, private residences, where centrally located within a two-mile cluster of the waterways, walking distance (Judd and Swanstrom, 2006). Goods were produced for local or regional production in small workshops or homes by skilled artisans, who employed one or two apprentices. The proximity of production and life was minimal. The Mercantile American city mirrored the European feudal enclave, and the communal nature of the social contract. Mass production, a key component of industrialization, was nonexistent. Labor existed within the workshop model of skilled or semi-skilled craftsmen, practicing closed father-to-son apprentice training. Industrialization interrupted the closed generational/kinship nature of skilled labor, mechanization, specifically, and led to the first retraction of the imagined socio-economic contract, what Polanyi (1944) described as the "Double-Movement," this chapter will highlight the dynamic changes in American labor and its adherence to the imagined proximity driven communal contract.

It was within this early dynamic that American labor/industrial regionalism began to emerge. The American South embraced the tenants of the agrarian republic and by extension, the communal contract, and the American North flourished within the dynamism of industrialization. In New England, the area between the Hudson and Potomac River basins, a rudimentary hand labor persisted on family farms, where the main seventeenth-century crop was Indian corn. The region also produced diversified crops such as wheat and other cereals on larger commercial farms. The larger commercial farms demanded labor, mostly supplied by European emigrees. In the American South, planters focused on producing specialized crops that were ripe for export (tobacco in Maryland and Virginia, and rice and indigo in South Carolina). Cultivating crops such as indigo, rice, and tobacco are labor intensive and necessitated a substantial labor force comprised of white-bound indentured laborers and black slaves.

Early American industry was organized to support American trade or domestically to support growing Eastern cities, whose economic health was equally tied to trade. Small-scale industry was organized to support maritime trade, but small-scale industries required both skilled and semiskilled laborers. Historian Richard Morris (1983, p. 12) writes:

> .... the [American] colonies established glass industries, brick and tile yards, and potters' kilns; bog ores proved suitable for making castings and hollow ware, and rock ores fed furnace and forge industries. A flourishing lumber industry supported related activities such as shipbuilding and the production of naval stores and potash. New England's white pine provided masts, yards, and spars for the Royal Navy; the white oak of the Middle Colonies supplied valuable stock for

the cooperage industry, and other hard woods of that area were used in the cabinetmaker's trade; in the South, yellow pine was the principal source of tar, pitch, and turpentine. Fishing and whaling required substantial fleets and thousands of sailors.

The thirteen American colonies were British possessions, and initially, the British encouraged settlement of the territories by their citizens. Both skilled and unskilled British laborers emigrated to the colonies; however, the thirteen American colonies were not freed from the extractive nature of colonialism, because they were settler colonies. We must recall the industrial revolution began in seventeenth-century England and flowed east across the European continent. It was the Scottish-born James Watt, who, in May 1765, added a condenser to a Newcomen steam engine, which increased the efficiency of the engine that would become the impetus of the industrial age. Gradually, England rose to commercial and industrial primacy by the end of the seventeenth century. Official English emigration policy changed, culminating in the enactment by Parliament in 1765 of a law forbidding the emigration of skilled workers and the statutes of 1774, 1781, and 1782 forbidding the exportation of textile machinery, plans, or models. The extractive nature of the British to their colonies can be observed by viewing *Figure 4.1*, which displays the one-way flow of raw goods from the colonies to the England.

Figure 4.1: Leading Colonial Exports, 1770.

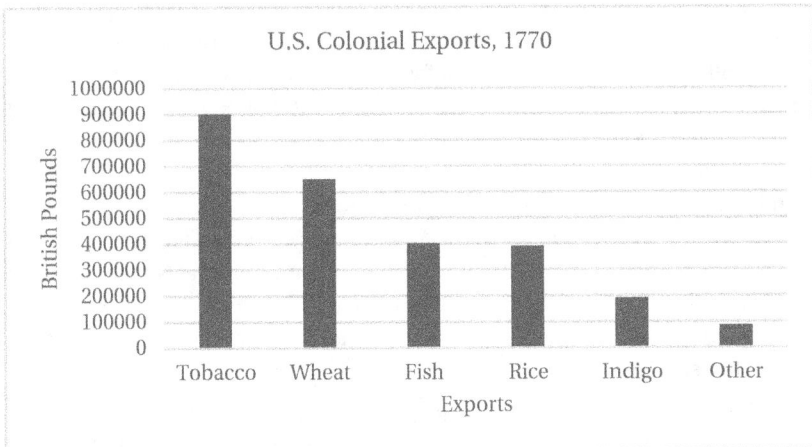

U.S. Colonial Exports, 1770

Source: U.S. Department of Commerce Bureau of the Census, Historical Statistics of the United States. Colonial Times to 19701: and Current Population Reports, Series P-23, Ancestry and Language in the United States; November 1979.

It should be noted that prior to the American war for independence, the British embargo on the emigration of labor did not extend to the poor or unskilled. The poor, the untrained, the vagrants, and the criminal class were encouraged to immigrate to the colonies utilizing indentured contracts, as a cost of travel. The embargo on skilled labor was confined to Britain, as skilled artisans from Europe flowed to the American colonies. Morris (1983, p. 14) writes,

> …Swedes came to the Delaware, Walloons and Dutch to settle New Amsterdam. To Virginia came Polish workers for the naval stores industry, French to cultivate vineyards, Italians to set up glassworks, and Dutch to erect sawmills. Georgia recruited Italians for silk culture; emigrants from the Germanies shipped out in large numbers to become farm workers and ultimately owners, to labor in the burgeoning iron industry, and to produce naval stores. Irish flax workers developed the linen industry in New England as well as on Maryland's Eastern shore. The Scotch Irish worked the far reaches of Pennsylvania and the Shenandoah Valley. In the lower South, sizable forces of Greeks, Italians, and Minorcans were transported to British-controlled East Florida.

The late seventeenth and eighteenth century would be a foreshadowing of the mobility of labor that was critical to the rise of American industrialization.

Seventeenth and eighteenth-century American labor scarcities led colonists to utilize several forms of bonded labor systems. As mentioned previously, indentured servitude was practiced throughout colonial America. The practice entailed all persons bound to labor for periods of years as determined by a written agreement, contract, or by the custom of the respective colony. Contract laborers were the most common immigrants. The system underwrote the transportation cost of European immigrants to the colonies, and in return, they bound themselves as servants for varying periods, but usually a length of four years. A second form of bonded labor freely practiced in colonial America was a debtor's bond. The English norm of the debtor prison was largely ignored in the American colonies and substituted with peonage. Colonial laws were enacted, releasing the debtor from prison to serve the creditor for a period of time sufficient to satisfy the debt.

An additional method of colonial labor was the apprenticeship system, which first arose from the medieval guild system. The model relied on highly skilled craftsmen to train young men in their trade. Traditionally, the system followed the communal model from father to son but binding out was not uncommon. It involved the voluntary or involuntary labor bond of fourteen-year-olds to master craftsmen, as free laborers in return for training within the craft.

It was the war for independence that spurred American manufacturing and the embryonic rise of labor. During the late seventeenth century, the British struggled to cover the rising costs of maintaining a global empire. The government rejected excessive domestic taxation and extracted the cost of maintaining a global empire to its colonies. In America, extractive taxes such as: the Sugar and the Stamp Act, Navigation Acts, Wool Act, Hat Act, the Proclamation of 1763, the Quartering Act, Townshend Acts and the Coercive Intolerable Acts, all infuriated British settlers, colonists. The colonist did not view themselves as living beyond the British social contract. The colonist viewed themselves as British subjects with all rights and privileges thereof, and the weight of the extractive taxes imposed without due representation in the British parliament, placed the white male colonist outside the norms of their defined social contract. Note that the slogan of the American independence movement was, "No taxation without representation."

King Cotton

Figure 4.2: U.S. Cotton Production 1790-1860.

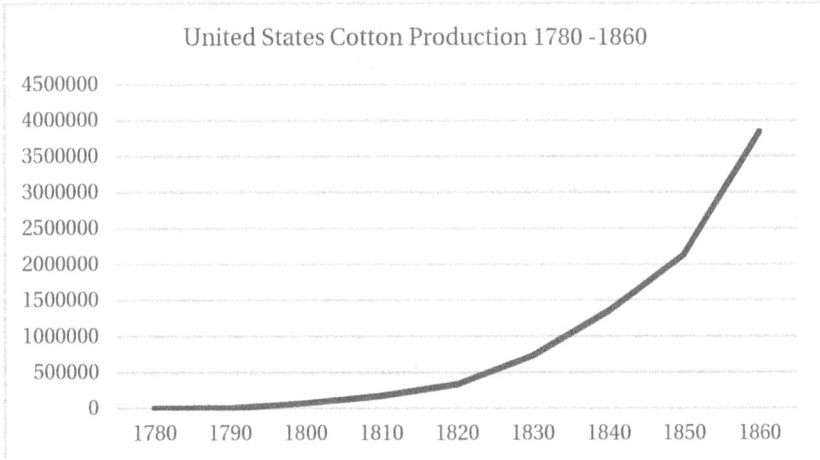

Source: Williamson, Samuel, Louis P. Cain. (2020). "Measuring Slavery in 2020 Dollars." *Measuring Worth.com:* https://www.measuringworth.com/slavery.php

The thirteen colonies were tied economically to the British with a majority of colonial exports flowing to England as displayed in *Figure 4.1.* The economic bond was further buttressed by the eighteenth-century expansion and demand for American cotton. Douglas North (1990) observed that cotton was the driver of American nineteenth-century economic expansion. The end of the American war for independence potentially impaired the fledgling economy, but the increasing European demand for cotton, which was buttressed by the British appropriation of Indian cotton processing techniques in the eighteenth century and Eli Whitney's 1793 invention of the cotton gin, became the driver of the American economic engine. *Figure 4.2* displays the steady increase of American cotton production from the beginning of the nineteenth century to the American Civil War. Cotton accounted for half of the American exports at the midpoint of the nineteenth century (Beckert, 2014).

A naval engagement on October 21, 1805, between the British and the French at the height of the Napoleonic Wars became an impetus of American industrialization. The British fleet led by Admiral Horatio Nelson destroyed the combined French and Spanish fleet. The victory gave the British naval supremacy, but the French controlled much of the European continent. With the French naval fleet destroyed, Napoleon initiated economic warfare on the European continent. On November 21, 1806, and again on December 17, 1807, the French implemented the Continental System, a pair of decrees that prohibited British trade with the Continent and threatened seizure of any neutral vessels found trading with England. The British responded by issuing the orders in council in November and December of 1807, which imposed a naval blockade on French-controlled Europe.

The United States remained neutral, with no significant naval fleet. The French seized American vessels docked in French-controlled ports. The British intercepted American merchant vessels at sea, both seizing cargo and impressing American seamen. America responded in 1807 with the Embargo Act, which halted British imports. The conflict eventually led to the War of 1812, but it had a second effect. The act placed an economic hardship on U.S. farmers and New York and New England mercantile interest, and it allowed French and English dealers, with surplus or smuggled supplies, of cotton to raise cotton prices at will.

The embargo spurred American embryonic manufacturing that was still tied to the exportation of raw materials to Europe. This was important, given that at the turn of the nineteenth century, American manufacturing was in its embryonic stages. The first American factory was built in 1790 by British immigrant Samuel Slater. He copied the milling process from factories in the United Kingdom and utilized the knowledge to organize America's first cotton mill, but American producers cutoff from European ports were forced to grow, and over the period of the war, American manufacturing increased. By the year 1816, United States capital investment in sugar refining, textile manufacturing, and other industries grew to one-hundred million dollars, and over 100,000 people were employed as factory workers (Weil, 1998. p. 1343)

The years after the American Revolution and the War of 1812 witnessed a further transition in American labor: the factory system spread, the transition from custom work to wholesale order work increased, and the concentration of workers in certain expanding industries increased. The transition was due largely to foreign competition, British imports. Over the period, the British dumped cheap imported goods in the American market, which forced American producers to adopt with cost-cutting devices, for example increasing the ratio of apprentices to skilled journeymen and to substitute the factory for the old domestic or putting-out system. However, the transition to the factory system required greater capital outlays than did craft shops or home manufactures, which limited many workers from acquiring the means to advance from laborer to employer.

The sociopolitical power dynamic was transitioning from the communal space to the anonymity of the factory floor. The means of addressing the imbalance faced by labor was collective action, the strike. The most suitable method of organizing collective labor action was the trade union. No legitimately organized American trade union appears until the first decades of the nineteenth century, but the transition or what Karl Polanyi (1944) coined the "movement" was in motion, but with the issue of forced labor, slavery, muting the transition until the 1870s.

Figure 4.3: Wealth Distribution 1860 North vs. South 2020 Dollars.

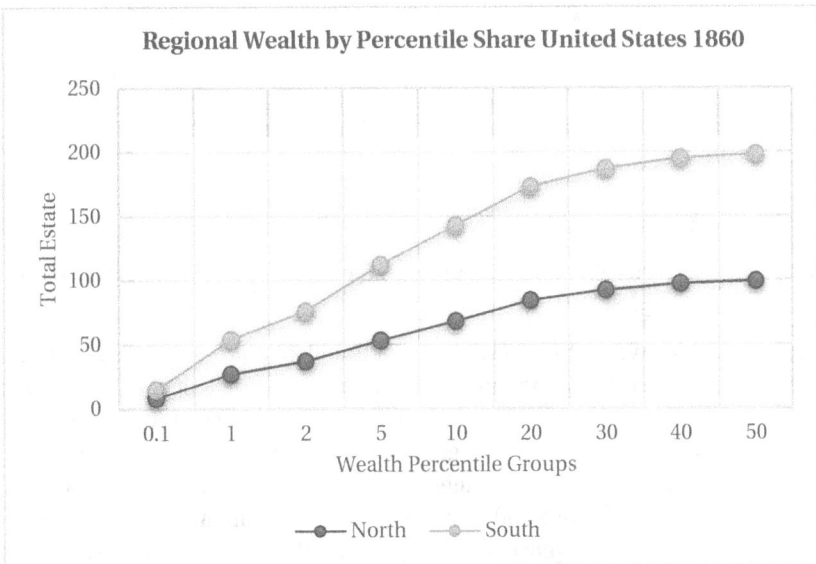

Source: Williamson, Samuel, Louis P. Cain. (2020). "Measuring Slavery in 2020 Dollars." *MeasuringWorth.com:* https://www.measuringworth.com/slavery.php

The period from American independence to the three decades that followed witnessed an American labor market that can be described as a sellers' market, labor was scarce, but it was marked by key regional differences, which can be interpreted, as both mobile, regarding domestic and international labor, wage restrictive, and tied to cotton production. The stark and regional American wealth disparity can be attributed to forced labor. The wealth of the southern agricultural states, which was bound to forced labor (slavery), outpaced that of the northern states, which is illustrated by *Figure 4.3* that displays the stark advantage in wealth held by the antebellum American South. In 1860, the American South was producing 75 percent of the world's cotton, and the Mississippi River valley held the highest concentration of wealth in the nation (Baptist, 2001).

Figure 4.4: The Correlation of Slavery to Cotton Production in the United States.

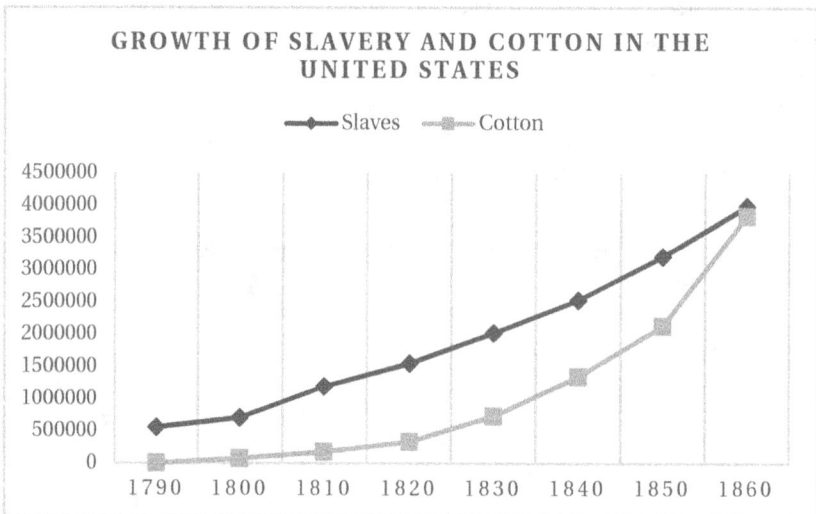

Source: Sven Beckert. (2014) Empire of Cotton A Global History, New York, Alfred Knopf.

Two factors converged to make America the ideal place to produce cotton, "...was our nation's unflinching willingness to use violence on nonwhite people and to exert its will on seemingly endless supplies of land and labor (Baptist, 2001, p. 1619)". The first great migration of African Americans took place at the beginning of the nineteenth century, and it was a movement from the Northeast to the South and Southwest. The arid climate of the American South made it an ideal place for the growing of cotton, and the increased world demand for cotton fostered the organization of large commercial farms, in the then-Georgia Territory. Slave labor became both the means and the embodiment of southern wealth, but the North played an equal role as primary points of embarkation for processed and unprocessed cotton and the centers of mercantile exchange focused on cotton exportation. The correlation of slavery and cotton production are displayed in *Figure 4.4*. Cotton accounted for half of all American exports during the first half of the nineteenth century; cotton served as national borrowing collateral for international loans; and it fostered dynamic domestic trade in agricultural products from the American West and manufactured goods from the American East. In two words, "cotton was the economic glue of the country."

Regional geography and socio-economic norms shaped the mid-nineteenth-century American economy. Hydropower was the key source of energy for early manufacturing, and locales with fast-moving rivers, which where the ideal locations for early manufacturing plants. Fast-moving rivers crisscross the northeastern United States and where the ideal locations for early manufacturing: mills, textile plants, and iron processing. Additionally, natural resource location dictated the rise of manufacturing hubs; the Pittsburgh-Lake Erie region has abundant deposits of iron, which fueled steel manufacturing in the area. In the South, where cotton was king, cotton mills were organized in greater numbers. By 1850, manufacturing and mechanized wage-incentivized farming was growing in the American North and West, but the South continued to rely heavily on agricultural production, cotton and sugar, utilizing slave labor.

Regional labor difference was amplified by the wage fears of free white male laborers. Manufacturing growth was well on the way to transforming the American economic system by 1850 with key indicators of labor transformations. In 1850, 57.3 percent of New York's free white men were employed in commerce or manufacturing, in contrast, Mississippi only witnessed 26 percent of free labor employed in manufacturing (U.S. Census Bureau, 2021). These differences in employment crossed into the American west with Ohio employing 53 percent of free white males in commerce or manufacturing (U.S. Census Bureau, 2021). The dynamic change in the American economic system was buttressed by the increased migration of Europeans to America.

In 1860, one out of every eight Americans were born outside the United States, and between the years 1820 to 1860, more than five million immigrants arrived in the United States. Most of the emigrees were Irish, German, and Jewish Eastern Europeans. Most of the immigrants, excluding the Germans, arrived without capital or skills. The Irish settled primarily in northeastern cities and towns performing unskilled labor. German immigrants, composed of mostly middle-class citizens fleeing political persecution, settled in

Midwestern and Western rural areas. The growing sector of wage laborers were politically and economically susceptible to forced labor, slavery.

The susceptibility was witnessed by the minor but influential rise of the Free-Soil Party. Congressman David Wilmot of Pennsylvania, in 1846, introduced the Wilmot Proviso bill. The bill would have prohibited slavery in the vast southwestern American territories. The bill neglected to garner enough support in the U.S. Congress but gave ideological impetus to the Free-Soil Party. Disenchanted members of the Whig Party met in Buffalo, New York in 1848 developing the party slogan, "free soil, free speech, free labor, and free men." The short-lived political party attracted small farmers, debtors, village merchants, and household and mill workers. The supporters shared a common interest, the fear and resentment at the prospect of black-labor—whether slave or free in the territories. The communal sphere that saw African Americans as the other and outside the social contract were the basis of post-reconstruction American society, but the end of the American Civil War, specifically, the ending of slavery assured the establishment of industrial capitalism as the dominant American economic system (Smith, 2017; Foner, 1975).

The Rise of American Unions: The Gilded Age

The post-Civil War period witnessed multiple efforts at American mass labor organizing, most notably the Knights of Labor. The Knights of Labor were founded in secret in 1869 and progressively welcomed unskilled, semi-skilled, and skilled workers. The organization also welcomed immigrants, African Americans, and women. The Knights of Labor was founded at the end of the socio-politically turbulent decade of the 1860s, but the following decade would be mired by both economic growth and upheaval. The upheaval and growth can be viewed within the dual context of Polanyi's (1944) "Double Movement," in which industrialist reorganized society into the wage system, at the expense of labor, only to have labor demand concessions; and for labor to retract to the communal proximity defined social contract.

The decade of the 1870s witnessed the United States economy grow at its fastest rate. Real wages grew, as American industrial output soared, which was witnessed by gains in U.S. gross national product, the demand for labor skyrocketed, and concentrated wealth was amassed. The American western prairie became the breadbasket of the world, with the output of wheat increasing by 256 percent and corn by 222 percent between 1865 and 1898 (U.S. Census Bureau, Historical Statistics, 1957). The increase in industrial output over the period was buttressed by an equal demand for fuel to power the expanding industrialized centers with an increase of 800 percent in coal cultivation, and a rapidly expanding transportation system, that witnessed an increase of 567 percent of railway track.

The end of the American Civil War left millions of unskilled African Americans available to work the burgeoning plants in America's rapidly expanding industrialized centers, but the opportunity afforded to both mobile domestic and international labor was not afforded to African Americans. Susan Breitzer (2011, p.69) asked the question, "…what made a worker an American worker, entitled to not only employment but also union protection…" The Gilded Age answer to the question was that not black skin color, and the demand for Gilded Age labor would be met by European immigration. The wave of European immigration was documented in the previous chapter, but the working and living conditions of factory work in the Gilded Age was deplorable.

Factory work hours ranged from ten to twelve hours per day and included Saturdays. Unsafe working conditions were the norm, not the exception. Pay was extremely low; child labor was common because of their size; it allowed children to fit in tight spaces in factories and mines. Within the decade of the 1870s, American wages decreased as GDP simultaneously increased (Foner, 1955, p. 17). During the decade, workers collectively began to exercise the power of the strike to deal with the conditions, and the response from employers was often to utilize impoverished newly arrived immigrants as strike breakers. Foner (1955, p. 17) writes that, "…the moment it appeared that a union was being formed and a strike prepared, the employers would introduce machinery and import unskilled labor to operate machines." In many cases, the newly arrived immigrants because of language barriers or miscommunication were unaware of the labor strife, and several instances witnessed newly arrived immigrant replacement workers joining the picket lines, with workers they were hired to replace. The overall employer strategy was successful, and only available in such a fluid labor market.

The Union Shop Movement Within the Captured State

The working conditions outlined in the previous section, and the underlying movement were highlighted by capitalist and legislative concessions. The state of Massachusetts passed the first American law requiring factory safeguards, in 1877. The trend continued throughout the year, with fifteen additional states passing work site safety measures, and by 1884 the United States Bureau of Labor was established. Labors wins in the legislature were quickly thwarted by the courts, in which much of the legislation was ruled unconstitutional. The "Yellow Dog" oath or the "iron-clad" was popularized by employers in the 1870s. It required employees to pledge against union membership, as a condition of employment. The pledges were court challenged in 1908 within *Adair v. United States*, 208 U.S. 161 (1908). The court ruled in favor of the plaintiffs but was careful to restrict the decision to the provision relating to discharge, thus, the court steered away from adjudicating whether "yellow dog" oaths were legal.

The most glaring example of the captured state was the court's interpretation of the 1890 *Sherman Antitrust Act*. The law was written by reformers, with the intent to curb the monopolistic practices of business cartels, and the law forbad any "restraint of commerce" across state lines. The initial instance of the court operationalizing the law against union action was in 1894. Members of the American Railway Union led by Union President Eugene Debs, walked off their jobs at the Pullman Palace Car Company located in Chicago, Illinois. The work stoppage spread across several states, with sympathetic workers joining in the action by refusing to handle Pullman railroad cars. The action brought the entire American railroad industry to a pause. The strike was a response to the Pullman's company strict administration of a company town and a cut in wages of up to 40 percent. A cartel of railroad magnates, including Pullman, pressured the court to issue injunctions, arguing that the work stoppage violated the provision of the Sherman Antitrust Act that forbade any "restraint of commerce" across state lines. The federal court agreed, enjoined the work stop issuing an injunction, and federal troops were mobilized to enforce the injunction.

The court-issued injunction became the tool utilized against union work stoppages. It must be understood that the primary collective tool of the worker in the employer-worker power dynamic is the strike. Courts siding with employers against the tactic effectively shifted the power dynamic solely to the employer. The consensus was that strikes involved picketing and sometimes violence, and the courts held that as a remedy an injunction could forbid violence, forbid the intimidation of non-union workers, or hold that any picketing was necessarily intimidating and unlawful.

The Knights of Labor advocated nationally for an eight-hour workday, and between April 25 and May 4th, 1886, their movement reached its zenith in Chicago, Illinois, where allied unionist, reformers, socialists, anarchists, and ordinary workers met to publicly advocate for the policy. Over the nine days of the event, organized marchers paraded through the streets, and thousands of attendees joined countless meetings. It culminated on May 1st, when 35,000 workers walked off their jobs in solidarity, and on May 3rd and 4th, attendees traveled from workplace to workplace pleading for workers to join. The events witnessed numerous clashes with the Chicago Police, with at least three shootings.

A long-simmering strike involving the Chicago-based McCormick Reaper Company erupted in violence on May 3rd, with police firing upon the strikers, killing two workers. The police violence infuriated the protestors, who called for a meeting to protest the violence at the West Randolph Street Haymarket.

A crowd gathered in the vicinity of the Haymarket during the evening of May 4th. After an inflammatory speech aimed at the police, the Chicago Police ordered the meeting to disperse. An unknown person hurled a bomb at the gathered police, killing one police officer and injuring scores of others. Police responded with gunfire killing an unidentified number of protesters, but eight police officers were killed and sixty wounded.

The aftermath of the event witnessed widespread hysteria directed against organized labor and immigrant workers. The Knights of Labor shouldered most of the blame, at the time, it was the largest national labor organization. The Knights of Labor's involvement in the riot was spurious; it had simply advocated for an eight-hour workday. Nevertheless, spurred by xenophobia and public mistrust many KOL locals joined the newly formed American Federation of Labor, led by Samuel Gompers (Glenn, 2002, p. 78-79).

The Knights of Labor at its zenith in the 1880s counted over 700,000 members. Of its membership, 60,000 were African American. "...John W. Hayes, Secretary of the Order, estimated that in 1886, when the membership of the Knights exceeded 700,000, there were no less than 60,000 Negro members" (Foner et al., 1968, p. 70). The Knights of Labor welcomed African Americans and gave complete autonomy to African American locals. In 1887, the New York *Sun* reported the existence of 400 all-black locals within the Knights of Labor, most of the autonomous locals located in the American South (Foner et al., 1968, p. 71).

The racial openness of the Knights of Labor owed to the attitude of its founders, Uriah Stephens and Terence V. Powderly. Stephens was a member of the American abolitionist movement, and he advocated for post-Civil War reparations for newly freed African Americans (Kessler, 1952, p. 250). Powderly viewed unionism as a universal tool for the worker against employer mistreatment regardless of race. Powderly (1882, p. 119) wrote, "...the policy of the trade union, and strikes, is what I am asked to explain. To the policy of the trade union is to protect its members against the encroachment of the unjust employer."

The rise of the American Federation of Labor after the collapse of the Knights of Labor was the impetus of the communal contract, within the American labor movement. Public opinion regarding organized labor was molded within the frame of the Haymarket Riot and America's constant undercurrent of xenophobia. Institutionally, the legal system was captured by anti-labor interests, and organized labor was forced to maneuver within the environment. Into this vacuum stepped Samuel Gompers and the American Federation of Labor.

Samuel Gompers was a second-generation cigar roller, the son of an English family that immigrated to New York in 1863. In 1864, fourteen-year-old Gompers joined the Local Fifteen of the United Cigar Makers Union. Ten years later, twenty-five-year-old Samuel Gompers was elected president of the reorganized trade union. During the 1880s, Gompers helped to establish the Federation of Organized Trades and Labor Unions, which would later become the American Federation of Labor, and in 1886 Gompers was elected its president.

The decade of the 1890s witnessed the American Federation of Labor grow to be America's largest labor organization under the direction of Samuel Gompers. It was Gompers, who modeled the American labor movement within the context of the union shop movement, with the advocation of craft trades unionism, which restricted union membership to wage earners and grouped workers into locals based on their trade or craft identification. This contrasted with the Knights of Labor, which had organized general, community-based organizations open to wage earners as well as African Americans and women. It also contrasted with the "one big union" philosophy of the Industrial Workers of the World. Second, the American Federation of Labor focused primarily on economic rather than political reform, adhering to political nonpartisanship, this contrasted with the labor movement in Great Britain and Germany, which dually focused on political and economic reform.[1] Ultimately, the focus of the American Federation of Labor would result in American labor's classification of one of many varied competitive interests in a plural political system.[2]

The union-shop system relies exclusively on proximity and trade. A proximity of production delineated to the factory shop. It focuses on organizing individual factories or workspaces into individual collections of workers. The organized workers will then negotiate collectively with the employer. The individual shops

---

[1] Gompers abandoned the apolitical beginnings of the AFL during the first decades of the twentieth century. It came during the administration of President Woodrow Wilson (1912–1920), when Gompers and the federation enacted much of their program and enjoyed their greatest influence. During World War I, Wilson appointed Gompers to the Council of National Defense, where he helped mobilize labor support for the war. Gompers also was crucial in convincing Wilson to craft a wartime labor policy that for the first time in U.S. history explicitly articulated government support for independent trade unions and collective bargaining.

[2] The Industrial Workers of the World, popularly known as the "Wobbles," was founded in 1905. The progressive founders were committed to organizing labor without regard to skill, skin color, gender, or immigrant status (Foner and Lewis, 1980, p. VII). Breitzer, (2011, p. 271) argues that the Industrial Workers of the World were viewed as too radical an alternative to the AFL for African American workers.

or trades can then join national or local organizations, like the AFL, that aid in organizing, negotiating, or managing individual shops. It follows the nonpartisan concept originally advocated by the AFL.

The proximity of trade and the condition of employment excluded membership to workers that toiled side by side, workers that resided in the same neighborhoods, and workers that practiced the same trade. The context of the union shop movement is within the boundaries of the communal contract and should be considered a retraction within the social contract. Simply, when American labor was confronted with dynamic change, rapid industrialization coupled with the rise of the wage system, the response was a vestigial contraction to the familiarity of the imagined communal contract.

The contraction of the social contract also extended along racial and gender lines. Whole groups of workers were excluded from the AFL, groups that were considered too difficult to organize or too easily replaceable—immigrants, women, unskilled, and minority workers (Breitzer, 2011, p. 270). Within the AFL, semiskilled and unskilled workers were consigned to "federal locals," which can be defined as quasi-industrial organizations. The federal locals were temporary organizations, with the intent of being merged with appropriate trade unions. The process left the unskilled and unassignable workers without any union protection (United Electrical, Radio, and Machine Workers of America, 1996, p. 16-17; Breitzer, 2011, p. 271). The federal locals answered directly to the international leadership and lacked the autonomy of other locals.

The autonomy of AFL locals allowed for racially restrictive practices aimed at African American workers. Many locals refused to organize African Americans altogether, and other locals restricted African American membership to auxiliaries and federal locals. The AFL's connection to skilled labor further excluded African American membership, within a system were entry and trade training were controlled by the same locals that prevented African American membership. The entry door for craft skilled labor is training, and African Americans were excluded from the training, which prevented entry into the trades.[3] Locals viewed African American workers as potential strike breakers or competition, but the reality was that for African American strikebreakers, it was an opportunity to work in trades that had been denied to them by unions. It was

---

[3] The original by-laws of the AFL disallowed the use of race as a barrier against membership within locals, but the by-law was subjugated by allowing locals to adjust their own entry requirements; therefore, allowing locals to wholesale exclude laborers based on racial origin.

within this system of the racial contract that W.E.B. Du Bois (1918) found that, in 1902, forty-three of America's national unions had no African American members and twenty-seven openly barred African American apprentices.

It would be a misnomer to believe that the American labor movement was unsuccessful in achieving concessions from both the state and employers. The American labor movement was successful in achieving; a cessation of excessive workhours, with the institution of the eight-hour workday; the ending of child labor; and the codification of work safety guidelines. However, theses concessions do fall within the context of Polanyi's "Double Movement," therefore, we can consider the success muted. The state remained captured by monied interest, public goods like healthcare and defined pensions, are relegated at the seminal level of the union shop, instead of being nationalized. These concessions are a product of the interest-level state of American labor. Labor did witness a brief zenith, in which a faux equilibrium was reached between the state, monied interest, the Great Depression.

The Wagoner Act & Quasi-Equilibrium

On October 29th, 1929, also known as "Black Tuesday," the New York stock exchange collapsed. The collapse of the New York Stock Exchange foreshadowed a decades-long world economic decline, the Great Depression. The context of the economic decline must be viewed in the socioeconomic changes that preceded it. The United States population was solidly urban, employment was waged based, economic inequality was extreme, the world economy was interconnected, and the American economy was industrialized. It was in the context of these socioeconomic dynamics that the world economy collapsed, and the United States and other Western countries grappled with the construction of a modern social safety net system.

On the verge of the Great Depression, American manufacturing was firmly centered in industrialized urban areas, but the decades-long northern business-centered Republican Party controlled the United States government. During consecutive, Republican presidential administrations, an anti-union sentiment permeated policy. The Republican presidential administrations of Warren G. Harding (1921-1923) and Herbert Hoover (1929-1933) operationalized their anti-labor policies, with refusals to adopt policies to recognize the right of collective bargaining; labor strikes were not protected by law; and arbitration rights between employees and employer were nonexistent.

The political and legal climate surrounding organized labor during the decade of the 1920s witnessed severe declines in union membership, which can be observed in *Figure 4.5*. Union membership during the decade was jeopardized by the "open shop." The open shop drops the requirement of employees in unionized shops to join or financially support unions. Financially, unions can collapse within an open shop system, as the free-rider effect, eventually leads to union financial insolvency. A second barrier to union membership during the decade was the economic suppression of unions by employers, with cash incentives directed at workers to prevent membership in unions, and the last barrier was the outright physical or violent coercion utilized to prevent union membership. Employers could utilize the various forms of anti-unionizing tactics because the state either advocated the practices or was simply captured by monied interests. For instance, when workers engaged in strikes, they often faced arrest or replacement by scab workers; and when violence erupted, the workers were the usual subjects of arrest.

Figure 4.5: Percentage of American Union Membership, 1880 to 2000.

Source: Bureau of Labor Statistics, U.S. Department of Labor, *The Economics Daily,* Union membership rate 10.5 percent in 2018, down from 20.1 percent in 1983 at https://www.bls.gov/opub/ted/2019/union-membership-rate-10-point-5-percent-in-2018-down-from-20-point-1-percent-in-1983.htm

The environment for organized labor during the decade that preceded the Great Depression was bleak, but the socioeconomic environment had changed. The decade of the 1920s was the first in which the American urban population surpassed the rural; the population changes are outlined in *Table 4.1* (U.S. Census Bureau, 2021). This is important because it signifies that the

American population was not predominantly rural and agricultural, and that survival during economic decline could not be solely subsistence farming. A second dynamic change was the reliance on manufacturing; manufacturing contributed almost all—eighty-three percent of the growth of the total factory production in the United States private non-farm economy between 1919 and 1929 (Field, 2006, p. 203). This is significant because it demonstrates that the American economy was firmly industrial-centered.

Table 4.1: Rural and Urban American Population 1860-1920.

Year	Rural	Urban
1860	25,226,803	6,216,518
1870	28,656,010	9,902,361
1880	36,059,474	14,129,735
1890	40,873,501	22,106,265
1900	45,997,336	30,214,832
1910	50,164,495	42,064,001
1920	51,768,255	54,253,282

Source: U.S. Department of Commerce Bureau of the Census, Historical Statistics of the United States. Colonial Times to 19701: and Current Population Reports, Series P-23, Ancestry and Language in the United States; November 1979.

One of the key issues that preceded the Great Depression was economic inequality. During the decade of the 1920s, an increase in manufacturing, the rise of discretionary incomes, and an increasingly urban population ushered in consumerism which equally correlated to consumption. Manufacturing is tied to consumption in a reciprocal relationship. For example, a factory worker earns wages to manufacture toasters. A person employed as a waiter, utilizes his/her wages to purchase a toaster, and the imaginary factory worker utilizes a portion of his/her wages to purchase a meal at the restaurant where the imagined waiter is employed. Therefore, the wage of each worker supports the other. This simplified example illustrates the reciprocal nature of a consumer-based economy, but what happens when no one has money to purchase the toaster; there are no wages for the factory worker, and, in turn, he/she cannot buy a meal to support the waiter.

The Great Depression mirrored this simplified scenario. There was a capital scarcity, due exclusively to inequality. A few held most of the capital, and there were little opportunities to engage in the reciprocal nature of a commodity-driven economy: in 1928, the top one percent of United States families received

23.9 percent of all pretax income; and about 60 percent of all families made less than $2,000 a year, the then livable income for a family of five (Bureau of Labor Statistics, 2021). It was not a supply issue, as warehouses and farmers held surplus products and crops; there was no money to purchase. In 1933, at the zenith of the Great Depression, one out of every four Americans were unemployed; industrial production between 1929 and 1933 fell by 47 percent, and gross domestic product declined by 30 percent (U.S. Bureau of Labor Statistics, 2021).

The capitalist system teetered, and the possibility of widespread social unrest was a possibility. The realization that within capitalist economies that a genuine hazard exists during a downward economic cycle for wage earners, the aged, the infirmed, or the very young was obvious during the period of severe economic decline. The American, New Deal, response was the creation of the modern state, with rudimentary social safety net provisions. The second response involved redistributive policies aimed at direct worker relief, to be paid for by increasing the taxation on the rich, redistributive economic policy. This is illustrated by the increase of the marginal tax rate to its highest level of 94 percent in 1944; this meant that all income over $200,000 (with inflation equated to approximately $3.1 million in 2021 dollars) was taxed at the rate.[4] The last response was establishing an equilibrium between organized labor and employers, the Wagoner Act.

Senator Robert F. Wagner, a Democrat from the state of New York introduced the National Labor Relations Act, which passed into law in 1935. It is the most significant American labor legislation of the twentieth century, and it established the American government as the arbitrator of labor disputes. It established the legal right of most workers, excluding agricultural and domestic workers, to organize, join labor unions, and bargain collectively with employers. Agricultural workers were excluded, which owes to the political environment surrounding the passage of the legislation. The New Deal Coalition consisted of northern labor, western agriculture, and southern Dixiecrats. The latter of the two openly opposed the inclusion of agricultural worker protections within the law.

The law established the National Labor Relations Board, a five-member board, with the power to resolve labor disputes through quasi-judicial proceedings. Specifically, the NLRB is empowered to decide, when petitioned by

---

[4] It should be noted that the top marginal tax rate increased throughout the decades of the Great Depression, and the 1944 rate must be taken in context of a War economy and funding.

employees, if an appropriate bargaining unit exists. It empowers workers to conduct secret ballot elections for the establishment of bargaining units, with sanctioned protections against employer harassment.[5] The act prohibits employers from engaging in such unfair labor practices as setting up a company union and firing or otherwise discriminating against workers who organize or join unions. The act also barred employers from refusing to bargain with any such union that is certified by the NLRB, as being the choice of a majority of employees.

The law established a quasi-equilibrium between employer and employee, and the three decades that followed witnessed a zenith in American union membership, which was coupled with the American post-war industrial bonus. Provided with seminal protections, American labor union membership skyrocketed, over the period, and union membership reached its apex during the decade of the 1970s, which can be observed in *Figure 4.5* that depicts American union membership from 1920 to the present. The Wagoner Act provided a brief equilibrium between the power dynamic of worker and employee, but the act has inherent weaknesses; specifically, the act provides limited punitive punishments for employers that utilize retaliatory practices against organized laborers (Rhinehart and McNichols, 2021). Employers that practice retaliation against workers face no monetary penalties and workers receive no compensatory damages when subjected to employer retaliatory behavior; workers cannot pursue remedies outside the NLRB; and Workers who file cases before the NLRB do not get their jobs back on an interim basis while their cases are pending. This means workers whose rights have been violated can be out of work and losing pay for months and years.

The preceding weakness of the Wagoner Act was reinforced within the Taft-Hartley Act passed in 1947, by a conservative Republican Congress over the veto of President Harry Truman. The Taft-Hartley Act followed the precursors of anti-union norms of Coolidge and Hoover. It prohibited the closed shop, which precludes union membership as a condition of employment. It allows states to set provisions mandating that non-union workers not pay fees for the collective bargaining cost incurred by unions. It narrowed the scope of

---

[5] The Wagoner Act's constitutionality was challenged within the Supreme Court by *National Labor Relations Board* v. *Jones & Laughlin Steel Corp.* (1937). The suit alleged that the law unfairly intruded on the "freedom of contract" of employers and employees and unnecessarily incorporated the Commerce Clause on business entities operating outside of interstate commerce. The court narrowly upheld the constitutionality of the law with a 5-4 majority.

unfair employer labor practices and defined unfair union practices.[6] Union membership reached its high-water mark during the mid-1960s, and during the 1980s witnessed a precipitous decline. The weaking of the Wagoner Act is one of the variables in the decline, but it is only one. Other variables include the marginality of labor as one of many interest groups in a pluralist system, the transitioning American economy, and the attachment of labor within a political coalition to a regionally southern agrarian political party.

Labor and the Party of Dixie

The New Deal Coalition successfully wielded political power from 1932 to the late 1960s. President Franklin Roosevelt masterfully organized seemingly differing geographically distinct factions, western agriculture, northern labor, and southern Democrats, "Dixiecrats," into a successful governing coalition. The coalition game together at the height of the Great Depression, in what some scholars describe as a realignment of the American electorate into a weak class-based cleavage (Key, 1955; McRae and Meldrum, 1960; Campbell et al., 1960; Shively, 1972). The most dominant faction within the coalition were the southern Democrats, and southern Democrats originated from an agricultural region steeped in race-based politics (Key, 1949). Labor primarily existed in northern large urban centers, Chicago, New York, Philadelphia, St. Louis, Detroit, and Boston. The 1935 passage of the Labor Relations Act came a year after widespread protest, with the failure of National Industrial Recovery Act, and liberals were able to push through the measure, with obvious concessions to southern and western agricultural interest, the exclusion of agricultural workers (Skocpol et al., 1990). This foreshadowed labors relationship with the southern element of the Democratic Party, which regionally lacked any historical ties or foundations with labor interests.

The Wagoner Act was influenced by the southern and western elements of the New Deal Coalition; elements that maneuvered to exclude agricultural labor from the benefits of collective bargaining: the ability to collectively negotiate better wages, safer work environments, and other fringe benefits of employment (healthcare and pension benefits). The National Labor Relations Act protects these bargaining rights for defined workers, but not agricultural workers. The southern and western factions of the New Deal Coalition

---

[6] The Wagner Act was further amended by the Landrum-Griffin Act (1959), which banned secondary boycotts and limited the right to picket. In *Janus v. American Federation of State, County, and Municipal Employees* (2018), the U.S. Supreme Court invalidated the agency shop for all public-sector employees.

represented agricultural reliant regions and negotiated to protect their regional agricultural interests from the collective demands of labor.

The congressional seniority system favored agricultural interests, with southern Democratic congressmen chairing the powerful Ways and Means Committee for the majority of the decades of the 1950s through the 1970s. With control of the powerful committee, and an increasingly powerful "iron triangle" of interwoven policy interest groups, elected officials, and bureaucrats that favored policies that included price supports and subsidies for agriculture. However, the "Yellow Dog" southern Democrats displayed little to casual interest in supporting pro-organized labor interest over the same period. A competition arose between dueling interest groups vying for entry and positive outcomes within the policy stream, northern labor and southern and western agriculture.

The interest group policy played out in Southern California with the emergence of the National Farm Workers Union during the late 1960s and early 1970s. The National Farm Workers Union was organized by labor/civil rights activists Cesar Chavez, Dolores Huerta, and Gilbert Padilla in 1962, a similar organization, the National Farm Labor Union, was organized in 1946, but without the institutional support of northern progressives or organized labor. The Wagoner Act does not offer the adjudication rights defined in the act to farm workers, but it does not prevent farm workers from forming unions and the practice of collective bargaining; and the United Farm Workers goals were in line with organized labor: to secure work contracts with large commercial agricultural enterprises.

There were obvious obstacles the NFW faced, with a majority of potential members identified as Mexican American migrant workers: the first obstacle was a weak bargaining position, with no statutory collective bargaining protections; farm workers existed in a system of poverty and a culture of resignation; there were high rates of migrancy and weak social cohesion, and a perpetual supply of farm labor, which insured that growers could break any strike (Jenkins and Perrow, 1977, p. 249). The National Farm Workers were aided by organized labor; specifically, the Teamsters and northern progressives (Dray, 2010, p. 570). The NFW received its first collective bargaining contract in 1966, with substantial pressure placed on the grower by supportive Teamsters. The support came from both northern progressives and organized northern labor to stifle the strangle hold agriculture had on southern Democrats and to empower organized labor's influence in the policy stream.

The context of the American labor movement must be viewed within the macro elements of the world economic system, America's racial context and the adherence to the racial contract throughout American institutions, including political and labor institutions, and the interest group adherence of organized labor within the American political structure, with all these elements culminating in the late 1970s and early 1980s contraction of the American labor movement. A popular lament is that the following factors led to a decline of the labor movement during the 1980s: economic restructuring, the decreasing credibility of liberal policies, increased business spending on campaign finance and political mobilization, greater suburbanization, the growth of the Reagan Democrats among union voters, public animosity toward special interests, and Republican presidential victories (Dark, 1996, p. 83). The preceding factors are not necessarily in error, but can by synthesized into two primary factors, increased globalization, and the amplification of the racial contract.

Let us examine the latter first, the amplification of the racial contract. Thomas Frank (2004) examined the exodus of former Democratic Party voters for the Republican Party in the State of Kansas during the 1980s, and he concludes that the mobilization, which sometimes contradicted with economic interests, was primarily over social issues, almost exclusively abortion. Frank's conclusions are not in error, but Frank too easily discounts the racial contract within his conclusions. Key (1949) formulated the "black threat hypothesis," in which he correlated the strength of southern Democratic partisan attachment to the proximity of white voters to African Americans. During the 1980s, the state of Kansas did not have a high concentration of African American voters; therefore, one could discount the proximity basis of the "black threat hypothesis," but 1980 was not 1940. Appeals to the racial contract were not exclusive to proximity but had reached the national and imagined locus of the social contract and were embodied within the underlying political ideology of conservatism. Ronald Reagan's 1979 opening campaign speech in Philadelphia, Mississippi was not simply a regional appeal to disaffected "Dixiecrats" it was a national appeal within the context of the racial contract.

The southern wing of the Democratic Party abandoned the New Deal coalition, and it abandoned the coalition exclusively over the racial contract, southern Dixiecrats became Republican Dixiecrats; however, northern labor remained at the institutional level attached to the Democratic Party. Afterall, in the American system, labor is not an organized political entity; it is one of many interest groups vying for entry into the policy stream (Kingdon, 1984). Western agriculture, not historically beholden to the New Deal, as the "iron triangle" of agricultural interest permeated both political parties, and conservative appeals for the imagined racial contract found willing ears in individual white Western agricultural states, including Kansas. Successive

Republican presidents, beginning with Ronald Reagan, retooled the Coolidge and Hoover anti-union norms of advocating for the open shop, weakening the National Labor Relations Board, and with Reagan's firing of the striking 1980 air traffic controllers a tacit nod to the employers that the tool of the strike was not a viable strategy for labor further weakened organized labor.

Appeals to the racial contract were also a factor in northern union members supporting Ronald Reagan in 1980 and successive Republican presidential candidates. Martin Luther King Jr. was assassinated in Memphis, Tennessee, in 1968. He was not in Memphis to protest Jim Crow laws; he was in Memphis to support striking sanitation workers, mostly African American. Most of the workers were so badly paid, that 40 percent qualified for public assistance (Isaac et al., 2006). A fact that displays that as late as 1968, African American laborers faced discrimination externally and internally from fellow laborers. Fellow laborers that railed against the prospect of working within the proximity of African Americans. Within the next chapter, globalization will be outlined, and globalization is important in explaining northern union members acceptance of the racial contract. However, the history of locals excluding or limiting African American members has been outlined, and at the height of the labor movement opening African American membership into local unions was often as the result of court action.

Paul Frymer (2003, p. 483) writes that in 1935, the year of the passage of the National Labor Relations Act, that African Americans only comprised 50,000 of all union members in the United States, and by 1985 that number had climbed to three million. Over the period, African Americans confronting continued union and corporate discrimination sought redress through several court cases under Title VII (Equal Employment Opportunity), of the Civil Rights Act of 1964, which prohibits discrimination in employment because of race, color, religion, sex or national origin (Frymer, 2003, p. 484). In *Quarles v. Phillip Morris*, 279 F. Supp. 505,515 (E.D. VA,1968) the state court held that plant/union seniority requirements in promotions were unlawful when it adversely affects African American workers. Similarly, in *Griggs v. Duke Power Company*, 401 U.S. 424 (1971), the Supreme Court ruled that entry-level local union membership requirements were designed to exclude African American membership and were violations of Title VII of the Civil Rights Act. In the case of the *International Brotherhood of Teamsters v. U.S.* 324 [1977] and the *United Steelworks of America v. Weber*, 443 U.S. 193 (1979), the court rejected a challenge of reverse-discrimination at the Kaiser Aluminum factory, where at the time only 2 percent of the unionized workforce was African American. The firm set-up a training program, with a set aside of 50 percent of the spaces for African American candidates. A white non-successful applicant sued arguing that he was immensely more qualified than several of the African American candidates that were accepted into the program, and, therefore, the victim of discrimination.

Northern white labors were as susceptible to the imagined appeals of the racial contract as any other group, and the historical barriers placed on African American membership in local unions supports the supposition. The effects of globalization were taking hold in the late 1970s, and disaffected white northern laborers, Reagan Democrats, gravitated to the appeal of the racial contract. It was rooted in the black worker as the other, and as potential rivals within a dwindling job market, that, for the first time in American history, was only dynamic for the highly skilled and educated worker.

Conclusion

The rise of the American labor movement is interwoven with technological advancement and social changes. The movement from hand production to mechanization and from the apprentice shop to the factory floor. The movement has a duality. One, it appears to break the initial bounds of the communal contract that were tied to the father/son kinship bond of apprenticeship. It is essential that we recognize that apprenticeship is located within the primary connection of kinship. A movement to the factory floor breaks the bonds of the seminal kinship model, with its placement of non-skilled and non-family members alongside one another on the production floor.

The proponents of the American agrarian republic focused on an adherence to the vestiges of the feudal agrarian production (the feudal social contract), with its ties to slavery and its rejections of key tenets of the liberal creed, but the world in the eighteenth century was organizing itself within the duality of industrialization and capitalism (Wallerstein, 2004). The evolving world and the conclusion of slavery witnessed American production switch to the industrial model, with a mass movement to urban centers and a reconfiguration of the social contract from the communal. The worker was a member of the proletariat and relied on wages for survival and the good will of employers. Employers motivated by profit, were not necessarily altruistic and the "double movement," although muted in America was initiated (Polanyi, 1944).

The American labor response was tempered by the captive state, with monied interests controlling key political and judicial institutions, and American labor retracted to the proximity of the communal contract, with an embrace of the proximity-based union shop movement. Minor concessions were met, but it reduced American labor to one of many interest groups vying for entry into the policy stream. The woes of the Great Depression resulted in a quasi-equilibrium between American labor and monied interest, with the passage of the Wagoner

Act in 1935, but it was only a respite to be broken by labor's coalition within a faction controlled by southern Democrats—a regional faction of the Democratic party, with little interest in northern factory workers, with strong adherence to the racial contract. The onset of globalization, the abandonment of the southern faction of the Democratic Party for the Republican Party to openly embrace the racial contract, and disaffected northern white workers' embrace of the racial contract left the American labor movement in contraction at the end of the twentieth century. In the next chapter, we will focus on globalization, and its sociopolitical response, the contraction of the social contract into the imagined communal state.

Chapter 5

Proximity, Nationalism, Globalization, & the Dynamic Social Contract

"Where globalization means, as it so often does, that the rich and powerful now have new means to further enrich and empower themselves at the cost of the poorer and weaker, we have a responsibility to protest in the name of universal freedom."

Nelson Mandela

Defining the term globalization is not a simple task. Theodore Levitt (1983, p. 92) was the first to use the term, and if we dissect the word, its root is globe, to encompass the entire world. A dictionary definition of the term "globalization" assigns an action status to the word, a verb, as a continuous transnational process of interconnectedness (Beck, 1997). Thomas Friedman (2005) embraces the preceding definition and asserts that expanses in technology have cemented an ever-increasing economically interconnected world. Jeffrey Sachs (2006) argues that the technology and interconnectedness embedded within globalization offers a potential *pareto* effect to mitigate poverty, but others have argued that globalization merely describes the world's economic system. James Dator (et al. 2006, p. 13) writes,

> For us here, globalization means not only the worldwide capitalist system called 'neoliberalism,' but also the full range of forces and factors that are sweeping across the globe totally unhindered, or barely hindered, by the boundaries and policies of the nation-state.

Ronald Chilcote (2002) argues that globalization is merely a retooling of imperialism. Chilcote (p. 80) writes, "…globalization is a politically motivated concept of ideological rhetoric centered on the notion of the evolution of harmonious and integrated world order to mitigate the tension and conflict that historically has disrupted the international political economy." The genesis of Chilcote's conclusion is embedded within Marxist theory. Marx and Engels predicted an expanding international market: "It must nestle everywhere, settle everywhere, establish connections everywhere" (Marx and

Engels, 1958, p. 37). Milojevic (2006, p. 76) adheres to a similar vein, with a declaration that globalization is the product of Western hegemony and patriarchy. Notwithstanding the preceding, global trade and production increased at levels never witnessed and can be illustrated by the growth of international trade, which can be viewed in *Figure 5.1*.

Figure 5.1: Index of World Trade Value, 1800-2014 (Values correspond to world export values indexed at 1913=100).

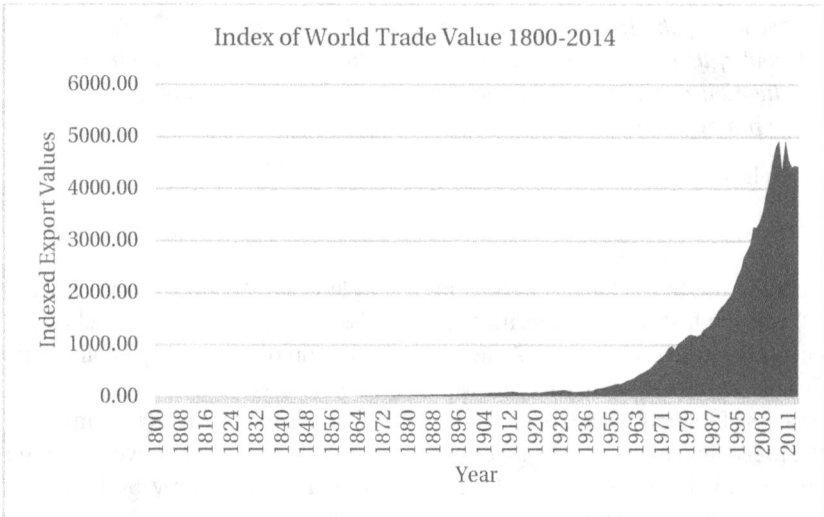

Source: Federico, Giovanni and Antonio Tena-Junguito (2016 b). 'A tale of two globalizations: gains from trade and openness 1800-2010'. *London, Centre for Economic Policy Research.* (CEPR WP.11128). https://e-archivo.uc3m.es/bitstream/handle/10016/22354/wh1602.pdf?sequence=1

The debate over globalization is unsettled; however, there is no contention about the intensity of international economic connectiveness. Production has increasingly become less attached to national economic factors. Production is stratified, with component manufacturing crossing international borders. This is possible because of changes in economic factors and the triumph of the liberal creed. The American triumph over fascism, at the conclusion of World War II, witnessed America's ascendancy as one of two global hegemons, which was cemented with the strengthening of the world economic system, with the 1945 Bretton Woods Agreement (Wallerstein, 2004). The Western world and the economic devotees molded the world economic system within the framework of the liberal creed: laissez-fair transnational trade, open domestic markets, centralized banking, and a hardened international currency (the American dollar).

The three factors of production remain, land, capital, and labor; however, factor mobility is now transnational (excluding land and unskilled labor). Unskilled labor remains geographically static and constrained. Unskilled labor mobility is constrained by a global surplus and the opposing force of the high global demand for highly skilled technical or knowledge-based labor, which is highly mobile. Simultaneously, capital both species and asset-based capital that includes machinery, tools, and land—the implements of production, excluding land, are increasingly internationally mobile.

The dynamic factor changes examined within the context of the Stolper-Samuelson theorem (1941) highlight predicted outcomes. A simple explanation of the Stolper-Samuelson theorem is that there are winners and losers when a nation trades internationally. Domestically, the advantages of international trade are accrued disproportionally to advantageous (surplus) economic factors. For example, a nation engaged in international trade, with a surplus of capital and a scarcity of labor will witness capital gains and disadvantages for labor.

This study purports to examine the Unites States within the context of the dynamic social contract, and our simplified illustration of the Stolper and Samuelson theorem serves as a key explanatory framework. As illustrated in the previous chapter, the United States from its inception relied on mobile labor, immigrants, to fulfill industrial demands during the nineteenth and twentieth centuries. America was and is abundant in the factors of land and capital. The dynamic flow of European labor satiated the industrial factories and commercial agricultural farming. The dynamics of the social contract played out within the nineteenth and twentieth centuries, with the vilification of Irish and then Italian laborers, who were placed outside the norms of the social contract, as non-members. However, time, assimilation, and the adherence of the racial contract nullified the effects of the dynamic social contract—via the assimilation of European immigrants over time that shared white skin color. Yet, as the nation embraced globalization, during the decades of the 1960s and 70s the imagined social contract witnessed a contraction.

During the American post-World War II economic boom industrialization fueled unskilled labor wage increases coupled with high union membership. The social contract remained relatively static outside of blows emanating from the Civil Rights Movement. We must remember that America could not be the drum major of liberalism, while domestically practicing illiberalism. This must be taken as a variable in the acceptance of Civil Rights Era concessions during the period, but by the beginning of the decade of the 1970s, neoliberalism was beginning to upset the American social contract. The following hypothetical illustrates the effects of globalization or neoliberalism during the decade:

An eighteen-year-old white male born and raised in Michigan finishes high school in 1965. We will refer to him as John Doe. He immediately seeks and gains employment in one of many automobile plants once located within the region. Young John Doe earns a salary that immediately places him firmly within the American middle-class. Doe marries, purchases a home, and starts a family.

John Doe's lifestyle is comfortable, and he is a member of his plant's union. A decade passes and Doe and his fellow workers collectively conduct a work stoppage to demand higher wages and increased benefits. Doe's employer is forced to negotiate, because the cost of capital, machinery and the tools of production, is of greater cost than labor. The employer concedes, and the demands of the workers are met.

A decade later, it is 1985, and John Doe has been employed for two decades. However, due to technological advancements the capital costs of production, machinery, in no longer greater or equal to the cost of labor. Simply, the cost of moving production is no longer prohibitive, and moving production outside the boundaries of the United States is even less costly. The calculus is even simpler, the employer can shave millions from the cost of production by relocating the plant outside of the United States, and import finished goods, with little to no threats of import tariffs.

John Doe's employer closes the plant, leaving John and thousands of his fellow workers unemployed. A large percentage of regional manufacturers follow suit and leave the region and the country. John Doe and his fellow unskilled workers are immediately members of a large sea of surplus unskilled labor. A now middle-aged John Doe is socioeconomically challenged, and his family's middle-class status is jeopardized.

The liberal orthodoxy whispers to John Doe that short-term retraining will enable his reentry into the middle-class job market. John Doe is middle-aged, unskilled, and at least two decades removed from the end of his education. The shifting economy is knowledge and service-based, and short-term re-education will place John Doe within a job market, with potential wages at a fractional level of his former earnings. He is openly unreceptive to the appeals of the liberal orthodoxy.

John Doe's reaction is tempered by the dynamic social contract. Doe is oblivious or rationally ignorant of the macro socioeconomic environment and is open to appeals that constrain the social contract for an earlier imagined social order. Doe is receptive to racialized and xenophobic appeals and openly embraces an earlier iteration of the racial contract.

Our fictional account is easily transferred to a white male Reagan Democrat. It appears perplexing that the voter utility would fall within preferences for a policy maker that was dually anti-union and pro- laissez-fair, but for our fictional John Doe and many others like him, the appeals of the racial contract were rational. Voters like Doe embraced a retraction of the social contract for an earlier iteration. The familiar cues of the racial threat were embraced and replaced the reality of globalization (Zaller, 1992; Key, 1949). It was and is an embrace of the imagined nationalized socioeconomic existence from the competition of the other (Anderson, 1983).

Owners' Equity & the Invisible Worker

The variables that trace the contraction of the social contract lie within the fluidity of capital and the proximity of production. Within the interconnected international world economic system, capitol is borderless. Digitized capital flows from border to border seeking to maximize profit or owners' equity. The owners are placed at the apex of the financial pyramid and their economic status is not measured as income but as wealth. Thomas Piketty (2003) explores the historical continuity of Western and American wealth as related to generational inheritance, maintained by earned interest and owners' equity. Wealth is maintained at the expense of labor, whose place in the economic system is at its floor, as a trader of labor for wages. Income does not sustain wealth at the poverty or middle-class level; it only sustains living conditions. The wealthy are freed from the labor exchange, and their wealth grows as earned or compounded interest are taxed marginally, because earned interest is only quasi defined as income. The American wealthy elite are freed from the labor exchange and can exist as the generational country club set (Veblen, 1899).

The inequality of the system is easily illustrated within the progressive and regressive nature of the American taxation system. The American federal tax system is a graduated progressive system, with increases in income resulting in increases in tax rate. In theory, the lowest earners pay the lowest level of federal progressive income taxes, but within the American system of federalism taxation is a shared power. The central government imposes an income tax and at the lower levels of the government structure states and local governments share the ability to levy taxes. An often rejoinder made to critics of the American tax system, is that the wealthiest one percent pay a disproportional share of federal income taxes, 40 percent.

A key misconception is to exclude the disproportionate share of American income earned by the wealthiest 1 percent (Chait, 2021). America's top one percent earn a disproportionate share of total cross income, 21 percent, which equals the gross income for the entire bottom 20 percent of American wage earners (United States Internal Revenue Service, 2022). This only illustrates one component of the American taxing system and excludes the regressive component. States and territories have the power to levy income taxes, and most do; however, states and local governments also impose other regressive taxes: property, excise, and sale's taxes. Wealth ensures mobility, and the wealthy can avoid high state income taxes by relocation. For the poorest Americans, relocation is a non-factor, as progressive taxes on the poorest are small; however, the effects of regressive taxes can affect a higher share of their income.

The taxation of earned interest further highlights the inequality of wealth opposed to income. Utilizing the United States tax rates on earned interest (capital gains) and income one can compare the taxation of a person earning wages of $100,000 to a similar person earning interest on the same amount, the data for the example can be viewed in *Tables 5.1 and 5.2* that illustrate the American graduated tax rate by income and capital gains taxes. Federal income taxes for the $100,000 wage earner will equal the prescribed $14,751, plus an additional $3,270, which includes the tax of 24 percent of the amount over $86,375 totaling a federal tax of $18,021. For a similar $100,000 of earned interest, the tax rate is 15 percent for a total of $15,000. At the federal level, income earned from wages or salary are taxed at a 27 percent higher level. At the state level, nine states do not tax capital gains, and the states that tax capital gains range from 2.9 percent to 13.3 percent.[1] One can argue that everything will even out, as states impose a varying tax rate on capital gains, but the wealthy have a mobility advantage—the wealthy can relocate their legal residency to states with low or no earned interest tax, but wages and salaries are tied to the state of employment, which average about 5.25 percent.[2]

---

[1] The state of California has the highest capital gains tax at 13.3 percent, and thirty-one states tax capital gains as income, with varying states taxing capital gains as a flat tax.

[2] Forty-three states levy income taxes, and the following states have no income tax levies: Alaska, Florida, Nevada, New Hampshire, South Dakota, Tennessee, Texas, Washington and Wyoming.

Table 5.1: U.S. 2021 Tax Rate and Taxes Owed by Income.

Tax rate	Taxable income bracket	Tax owed
10%	$0 to $9,950	10% of taxable income
12%	$9,951 to $40,525	$995 plus 12% of the amount over $9,950
22%	$40,526 to $86,375	$4,664 plus 22% of the amount over $40,525
24%	$86,376 to $164,925	$14,751 plus 24% of the amount over $86,375
32%	$164,926 to $209,425	$33,603 plus 32% of the amount over $164,925
35%	$209,426 to $523,600	$47,843 plus 35% of the amount over $209,425
37%	$523,601 or more	$157,804.25 plus 37% of the amount over $523,600

Source: United States Treasury, Internal Revenue Service, 2022; https://www.irs.gov/privacy-disclosure/tax-code-regulations-and-official-guidance

Table 5.2: U.S. 2021 Capital Gains Tax Rate.

Tax	Capital Gains
0%	$0 to $40,400
15%	$40,401 to $445,850
20%	$445,851 or more

Source: United States Treasury, Internal Revenue Service, 2022; https://www.irs.gov/privacy-disclosure/tax-code-regulations-and-official-guidance

Owners' equity is further separated from income by time. Stock prices can increase dramatically, simultaneously expanding the holder's wealth, but this is not taxable income. It can be subject to a capital gains tax, if the holder chooses to sell, but why sell. The stock could increase in value increasing owner's equity or held as a transferrable asset, thereby sustaining wealth. The wage earner does not have the same choice of deferment. Again, income or wages are the purview of the laborer, skilled or unskilled, and the nature of owners' equity further incentivizes managers to increase owners' equity in the short term, at the expense of labor.

The Western economic system trains managers within the context of the accounting formula:

$$A = L + E$$
A = Assets
L = Liabilities
E = Equity (Ownership)

Fundamentally, the formula represents the relationship between assets, liabilities, and owner's equity. For each transaction, the total debits equal the total credits, and the formula should be bisected between liabilities, to the right, and equity, to the left. Conversely, an increase in assets will be related to a decrease in liabilities and an increase in equity. We can rearrange the formula as follows:

$$E = A - L$$

Modern managers are taught to decrease liabilities to increase owner's equity, and within the formula examples of liabilities include payroll expenses and *accounts* payable. Payroll is the same as wages, and we can extrapolate that modern managers are taught to limit wages, thus, labor by extension is classified as a liability. In the classical since, managers are taught to limit labor and it manifests in dollars: limit labor benefits, limit wages, and construct barriers to collective labor action that could strengthen the two preceding limitations. Owners incentivize managers within the context of the process by attaching managers' compensation to owner's equity.

The attachment of management compensation to owner's equity places management outside the realm of the wage earners or proletariat, and outside the communal social contract. The manager is incentivized within the short term to increase owner's equity and his/her own short-term compensation by attaching compensation to the value of company stock, ownership. Curiously, this short-term approach leads managers to discount the long-term health of corporations, as their compensation is correlated to the present value of company stock. The median 2019 compensation level of America's chief operating officers was $785,000 while the median salary of American workers was $34,250 (United States Bureau of Labor Statistics, 2022). Chief operating officers earn roughly 22.9 times the salary of the main-line workers in their corporations.

The duality of the short-term incentive structure of management and the liability status of labor can be viewed in the context of the following examples. Thomas Edison, the American inventor of the incandescent light bulb, founded the Edison Electric Light Company in 1878. In 1892, the newly incorporated General Electric Company acquired Edison Electric and its subsidiaries. By the 1980s, General Electric had grown to be not only one of the largest corporations in the United States but in the world. It's 1980 workforce was 411,000, and its subsidiaries produced a wide variety of products and services including: consumer goods, commercial goods, defense goods, and even commercialized media. In 1980, General Electric Stock was valued at $8.125.

John Welch Jr. became the Chairman and Chief Operating Officer of General Electric in 1981. Welch was the son of an Irish American working class train conductor and was a highly educated chemical engineer earning a doctorate from the University of Chicago. He began his professional career at General Electric soon after finishing his education as a chemical engineer, and steadily rose through the ranks of the company to be named chairman and chief operating officer in 1981. The 1981 closing stock price for General Electric was $9.5633; it was a 6.82 percent decline from its highest 1981 valuation, but it was an 11.69 percent increase from the previous year's average price. The General Electric 1981 dividend was $0.07.

Chairman Welch explicitly forecasted that his primary mission was the increase of owner's equity. Columnist Scott Tong (2020) wrote the following, which describes a pre-Welch-led corporation:

> Once upon a time, GE explicitly served many masters: workers, research labs and suppliers. And last in line for company revenues: share owners. According to a 1953 annual report from the company's department of employee and plant community relations, the company paid out 13 cents on each dollar in sales to taxes, 44 cents to suppliers, 36 cents to employees and 1 cent to plants and equipment. "General Electric share owners got the remaining ... 3.9 cents out of each sales dollar in dividends."

This changed under Welch, and the focus would strictly be owner's equity. Under Welch, General Electric's focus was owner's equity witnessed by a dramatic increase in dividend payments over the sixteen years between 1981 to 1997: the 1997 dividend payment for common stock was $0.35, a five-fold increase from 1981. Additionally, the 1997 closing stock price for General Electric was $195.6533, a 95 percent increase from its 1981 value.

Welch accomplished this on the backs of and the tattered remains of General Electric employees. He instituted cut-throat management policies that codified the annual termination of the bottom 10 percent of company managers, regardless of performance, and rewarded the top 20 percent with cash bonuses and stock options. He brutally downsized and exported labor, and by 1985 of the 411,000 employees he inherited 299,000 remained. Upon Welch's retirement in 2001, he received a severance package of $417 million. The brutal tactics helped to increase General Electric's market share and expand owner's equity but stands as a classical example of management-incentivized attachment to owner's equity.

The system is further incentivized by globalization or the world economic system. The formula is simple, limit liabilities, and increase owner's equity. Technological advancement has lessened the cost and the mobility of production (machinery) this has resulted in what can be termed hyper-capitalism. Owners are freed from the income system and are motivated by the ease of transnational capital flow. Their investment dollars flow to where labor is cheap and production is free of governmental regulation, the laissez-fair states or the captured states. Unskilled labor is non-transient and restrained by national or international barriers, while capital seeks the less costly conduits of production, nations with surplus unskilled labor and laissez-fair regulatory structures. Labor is reduced to the simple drudge of production and replaceable when labor costs increase. Unskilled labor, being relatively immobile, is left to the whims of the market. Further, the consumption of production is outside the purview or price point of the maker, the laborer. For example, the popular Apple iPhone is produced in East and Southwest Asia. The lowest 2022 retailed price model sales for approximately $800, while the average yearly manufacturing salaries for the following East and Southwest Asian nations are: Taiwan--$1,924, Vietnam--$6,204, and Philippine--$8,800.

Overall, the globalized economic system stratifies workers, managers, and owners into a stratified socioeconomic contract. The owners take the place of the hereditary elite, with wealth historically maintained by earned interest, which frees them from the labor dynamic, the leisure class (Veblen, 1899). The inequality materializes from the apex of the "leisure class" to the next class, the managers, with their compensated insensitive to increase owner's equity, and below the managers are the highly skilled internationally mobile knowledge-based salaried laborer. At the bottom, is everyone else. It is a transactional system, which leans toward socioeconomic inequality, with the top tiers overly compensated, with the surpluses of production, but it is maintained in America and the Western world by stoking conflict among the lower tiers by appeals to the imagined racial contract.

Conclusion

Within the realm of the imagined American social contract the socioeconomic variable is supreme. The captured state is mobilized for the protection and the maintenance of inherited wealth. Wealth that is maintained via earned interest and dividends. Wealth that is marginally taxed compared to wage earners. It is maintained by a dynamic social contract that places American labor within a duality defined by transaction costs, race, and the imagined other. Transaction costs are embedded within class: the social order dictates the level of economic surplus received—at its apex the hereditary wealthy owners; just below, the management class; below the management class are the highly skilled knowledge-based laborers; and at the floor, unskilled wage earners. The system is maintained by cementing the imagined strife of the racial contract.

The racial contract relies on the imagined social construct of race materialized as skin color or pigmentation differences. The American white working class is inundated by elite appeals casting the socioeconomic struggle as a two-variable game or a zero-sum choice (Zaller, 1992). It defines non-white status as outside the benefits of the social contract. Policies or collective socioeconomic actions that are cast as beneficial to the "other" are rejected, with the zero-sum calculus—that any potential benefit awarded to the other potentially disrupts the social order, the racial contract.

Chapter 6

Proximity and the Racial Contract

"White supremacy is the unnamed political system that has made the modern world what it is today."

Charles Mills

The following 1963 quote from African American writer and scholar James Baldwin highlights the racial contract from the perspective of African Americans,

> The situation in Alabama and Mississippi which is spectacular and surprises the country is nationwide. Not only could it happen in Florida, it could happen in New York or Chicago, Detroit or anywhere there's a significant Negro population. Because until today, all the Negroes in this country in one way or another, in different fashions, North and South, are kept in what is, in effect, prison. In the North, one lives in ghettos and in the South, the situation is so intolerable as to become sinister not only for Mississippi or Alabama or Florida but for the whole future of this country.[1]

The words remain prophetic. In the roughly sixty-year span between Baldwin's observation, American has made political strides: twice electing an African American to the presidency; electing a woman of color to the Office of the Vice Presidency; and expanding minority representation in Congress. But dually American voter restriction laws aimed at hampering minority suffrage have passed in many of the old states of the confederacy harkening to a reconstruction of Jim Crow era voting laws, and the long-engrained socioeconomic problems of race persist: the African American unemployment rate is double that of whites; the incarceration rate of African Americans outpaces that of whites; the college graduate rate of African Americans lags that of whites; the life expectancy of African Americans trails that of whites; COVID infection and death rates of African Americans outpaced that of

---

[1] From "Florida Forum" on WCKT-Miami in 1963.

whites; the infant mortality rate of African Americans surpasses that of whites; the asset gap between African Americans and whites is vast (Minor, 2008). The African American epic is fraught by disenfranchisement and oppression, but to understand the socioeconomic climate of America, one must understand that politics and social order are dictated by race, and that it plays out through space. The previous chapters briefly outlined the context of the American racial contract. This chapter will focus on the proximity of the racial contract within the context of economic, political, and social outcomes.

The American Racial Contract Explained

Commensality places a negative social cost upon interactions with those outside the social order within the scope of everyday interactions, and commensality is a key component of caste. It castigates a social order outside the context of class, the poor, the middle, and the wealthy; and defines a fourth designation. A designation that revolves from a framework developed by Charles Mills (1997) that views the formation of the social contract via the lenses of "white privilege" or skin color. It is based on an Enlightenment-era formulation of the social contract that entailed a tacit codification defining the interactions and transaction costs between fellow citizens for collective self-interest. Mill's framework, the racial contract, details the exclusion of non-Europeans from the bonds of tacit rules regarding interactions and transaction costs between individual citizens. It designates white skin color as the designee of membership and rights and is more akin to the Indian caste system, and African Americans are at the floor of the American caste system, the untouchables. Social order, politics, education, and geography are played out through the lenses of race.

America's initial treatment of African Americans began as an imported forced agrarian workforce. The Agrarian nature of American slavery mirrored the then-dying land-based agrarian workforce of Western Europe; the captive African workforce were tied to land within the bounds of a strictly stratified social system with African captives at the floor and wealthy white landowners at the apex; and status was based on birth. The Civil War was a conflict within the context of the racial contract in which Americans openly struggled with the expansion of the racial contract within the bounds of an increasingly post-feudalistic market-based society in which labor was openly traded for wages. The ending of slavery witnessed a second reformation of the racial contract in which an American race-based caste was constructed, which remains at the heart of American sociopolitical interactions and transactions.

Before understanding Mills' framework, one must understand the context of Mills' racial contract. The racial contract has its foundation in the work of Carole Pateman (1988). Pateman explored the seminal question of contract theory from the feminist perspective and argued that contemporary scholarship ignored the role of gender domination, specifically, the sexual contract, that historically justified the governance of women by men. She explored the legal codification of the domination, which is modernly manifested via the institutions of marriage and employment. Marriage and employment, both legal abstracts that are defined by contract obligations. The initial marriage contract places women as the singular and contractually obligated property of men creating a codified relationship of domination and subordination.

Mills expanded on Pateman's earlier exploration arguing, "… that European expansionism and the establishment of white/nonwhite relations of domination could be seen as a similar constitution 'race' as a structure of exclusion (Pateman & Mills, 2007)". Mills argued that the original conception of the social contract was neither egalitarian nor inclusive and regarded, "…people of color (Native American and Australian) as savages." Mills rests his framework on the following three premises:

> …the existential claim—white supremacy, both local and global, exists and has existed for many years, the conceptual claim—white supremacy should be thought of as itself a political system, white supremacy can illuminatingly be theorized as based on a "contract" between whites, a Racial Contract.

On February 1, 1960, four college students, Joseph McNeil, Franklin McCain, Ezell Blair Jr., and David Richmond conspicuously took seats at a lunch counter of a Woolworth's store located in Greensboro, North Carolina. The act, on its service, appears to have been innocuous, but it was an open act of revolt against the tenants of the American caste system. The four college students were African American and service within the business followed the strictures of commensality, it was designated for whites only. The act of quiet defiance was met by their subsequent arrest, but it served as a catalyst for similar protests that would follow. In 2009, sixty African American children paid entry to a private swimming club in suburban Philadelphia when a witness advised of the following: "When the minority children got in the pool all of the Caucasian children immediately exited the pool," Horace Gibson, parent of a day camp child, wrote in an email, "The pool attendants came and told the black children that they did not allow minorities in the club and needed the children to leave immediately" (NBC News, 2009).

An Alabama Jim Crow era law read, "Every employer of white or Negro males shall provide for such white or Negro males reasonably accessible and separate toilet facilities." A similar Florida law of the era read, "All marriages between a white person and a Negro, or between a white person and a person of Negro descent to the fourth generation inclusive, are hereby forever prohibited." A Georgia law of the period read, "The officer in charge shall not bury, or allow to be buried, any colored persons upon ground set apart or used for the burial of white persons."

The Indian word "jati" describes the hereditary social structure of Indian society, which is described by the Portuguese word for race, casta. Indian society has four distinct social class categories, varna. At the apex of the system, are the Brahmins and at its floor are the untouchables. Physical contact between the upper classes and the lowest class was strictly prohibited, and Brahmins adhered so strongly to this rule that they felt obliged to bathe if even the shadow of an untouchable fell across them (Mabbett, 1977, p. 430). For the Indian caste system, there was no hope of social mobility individuals were born into, worked, married, and died within these groups.

Humans are invariably born with differing physical attributes, which once was attributed to human subcategories of race, which scientists have found are nonexistent, "Human evolution has been and is characterized by many locally differentiated populations coexisting at any given time, but with sufficient genetic contact to make all humanity a single lineage sharing a common evolutionary fate" (Templeton, 1998, p. 632). There are no human subcategories of race, only morphological differences: skin color, nose, and eye appearance etc. The notion of racial differences plays into the conception of white privilege (or white skin privilege) defined as societal privileges that benefit white people in Western countries beyond what is commonly experienced by non-whites under the same social, political, or economic circumstances.

The aforementioned instances of once codified race-based American laws and the more recent experience of the young African American swimmers hints to an American sociopolitical system that is more akin to the Indian system with the obvious morphological differences between blacks and whites making the ease of propagating the system. W.E.B. Du Bois (1903) famously predicted that the problem of the twentieth century would be the problem of the nineteenth century, race. Du Bois was correct and his analysis of the racial problem being the social spur that pushed the nation into war in the nineteenth century and cemented social segregation for most of the next century, but a sharper analysis of the American racial relations will display a historical sociopolitical system, with whites perching themselves at the apex of the social pyramid and with people of darker hues of complexion at the lowest rung, the untouchables. The unconscious or conscious reliance on the American caste system cements white privilege and dictates sociopolitical ideologies and constituencies. Simply, the American sociopolitical system is propagated by a race-based social order that maintains its existence by an adherence to the sociopolitical precepts that reinforce white privilege by classifying African Americans as the perennial subclass, the untouchables, and as potential socioeconomic threats to the white middle or lower classes.

The American revolution was the rejection of the European social order with its reliance on a hereditarily defined socioeconomic order for an equalitarian-based republican society. America's geographic distance from its European overlords allowed a democratic tradition to take hold in American institutions: Virginia's House of Burgess, and legislative assemblies in Maryland, New Hampshire, Massachusetts, New York, Connecticut, Rhode Island, Delaware, Carolina, and New Jersey. The distance from European capitals enabled American institutions to develop free from the influence of traditional governing institutions that existed in European capitals. Most of the colonial institutions could levy taxes, muster troops, and enforce British common law. Britain acted as the central government, enacting foreign policy and other broader centralized government functions.

America, unlike European colonies in Africa, Asia, or South America population was dominated by immigrating Europeans. The American colonial workforce was not a forced indigenous population as in Asia or Africa, but was primarily composed of European immigrants their decedents, indentured servants of European ancestry, or enslaved Africans. Most free land-owning white men could vote to elect their local and colonial legislations.

The pre-citizenship rights of the white European settlers or colonist ingrained a pre-existing social order retained from the colonizing country, a social contract. The pre-citizenship rights of Europeans have foundations in the systematic ending of Western feudalism and the inception of the modern social contract (Mills, 1997, p. 11). Simply, rights of citizenship for colonists from England were expected and transferred to the English colonists. English common law and legal practices were the basis of the colonial legal systems: voting rights were strictly for landowning white males, jury trials, and other legal practices of English law were the norm. English colonists considered themselves to be English citizens and tacitly bounded by the social contract.

People of African ancestry first made appearances in the English colonies in 1619; a Dutch ship brought twenty-two Africans ashore to the British colony of Jamestown. It was not uncommon for poor European colonists to begin their life in America as indentured servants, which required a stipulated number of years of service by an individual to pay off a debt, which was normally passage to the colonies. During the seventeenth century, these years of service became perpetual for Africans, and the debate was not centered on the natural rights of human beings.

In 1700, Massachusetts Judge Samuel Sewall became embroiled in a legal dispute with fellow Judge John Saffin, over the fate of an African indentured servant whom Saffin refused to free. Sewall published the pamphlet *The Selling of Joseph a Memorial* in which he relied on Christian biblical scripture to lambast slavery as an immoral practice. In 1701, Judge Saffin responded with the pamphlet *A Brief and Candid Answer to the later Printed Sheet, Entitled,* the Selling of Joseph. Saffin argued that Christian scripture not only condoned slavery, but wrote,

> [God]…who hath Ordained different degrees and orders of men, some to be High and Honorable, some to be Low and Despicable; some to be Monarchs, Kings, Princes and Governors, Masters and Commanders, others to be Subjects, and to be Commanded; Servants of sundry sorts and degrees, bound to obey; yea, some to be born Slaves, and so remain during their lives…

The enslavement of Africans sat in place the American feudalist system, which was immediately at odds with the enlightened natural rights basis of America's government, but not at odds with an implicit social contract that Charles Mills (1997) labels the "Racial Contract." Mills (1997, p. 11) argues that the Western social contract, "… set formal or informal agreements or meta-agreements (higher-level contracts about contracts, which set the limits of the contracts' validity) between the members of one subset of humans" (Western Europeans). All sets of other humans, owing to phenotypical/genealogical/cultural differences, are outside the bounds of the European social contract; and for Western Europeans, "…the moral and juridical rules normally regulating the behavior of whites in their dealing with one another either do not apply at all in dealing with nonwhites or apply only in a qualified form."

Utilizing Mill's framework to analyze the rationale of Judge Saffin's legal argument is that he [Judge Saffin] was not bound to treat Africans within the same legal/moral context of the social contract as he would treat fellow whites. It is this contextual foundation that American neo-feudalism was established with land-owning whites at the apex and Africans at the bottom, the serfs. Yet an internal moral and philosophical conflict persisted as challenges to the exclusion of Africans from the social contract persisted. The internal conflict was satisfied by both compromise and legal definition. For America's first national election, only land-owning white males were allowed the right to cast votes and to stand for office, but the same legal document that provided the legal basis of the nation defined the legal status of Africans. A compromise was agreed upon to give the lightly populated Southern states a greater proportion of allocated seats in the House of Representatives by counting African slaves as three-fifths human, it outlawed the importation of slaves after 1808, but did not outlaw the practice. The three-fifths clause cemented the status of people of African descent in the lower level of the evolving American feudal system.

The American Civil War was a conflict that beginnings lie in the original compromises of the American constitution. The tradition of compromise regarding the continued practice of slavery was historically evident by the Missouri Compromise and the Kansas-Nebraska Act, but the Fugitive Slave Act and the Supreme Court's rejection of the historical context of compromise in its ruling in the Dredd Scott decision effectively pushed the country toward war.

The aftermath of the Civil War and the end of the Reconstruction period sat in motion the sociopolitical effectiveness of the black threat hypothesis, and defined ideological and political cleavages that remain at the heart of American politics, social interactions, and social class distinctions. The end of the Reconstruction era witnessed the construction of the socioeconomic system that defined America through two lenses: white and the white-defined social order for Americans of color. The system was legally and socially enforced segregation that was based on the separate but equal doctrine that defined interaction with African Americans as a social and legally sanctioned taboo. It buttressed white privilege by defining people of color as the perpetual underclass, and the "economic boogie man" reinforcing the political cleavage of middle-class and poor whites to one of the two political parties.

Proximity "The Racial Threat Hypothesis"

The examination is conducted within the context of space, and the American racial contract exists in political, social, and economic geographies. Where Americans choose to live has two dichotomous components, race and class. Americans reside in increasingly diverse communities, counties, municipalities, towns, and villages, but at the neighborhood level, Americans live in both class-delineated and racially homogeneous space (Baybeck, 2006; Jackson, 1985; Massey, 1987; Siskind, 2005). *Map 6.1* illustrates the racially heterogenous nature of an American city, St. Louis. *Map 6.1* dually depicts the racially homogenous nature St. Louis neighborhoods, with racially homogenous concentrations. In the past, *de jure* and *de facto* racism provided the strictures of residential space, but in the absence of statutory segregation, Americans continue to reside in racially homogenous enclaves.

Map 6.1: Chicago Demographic map by race, 2010

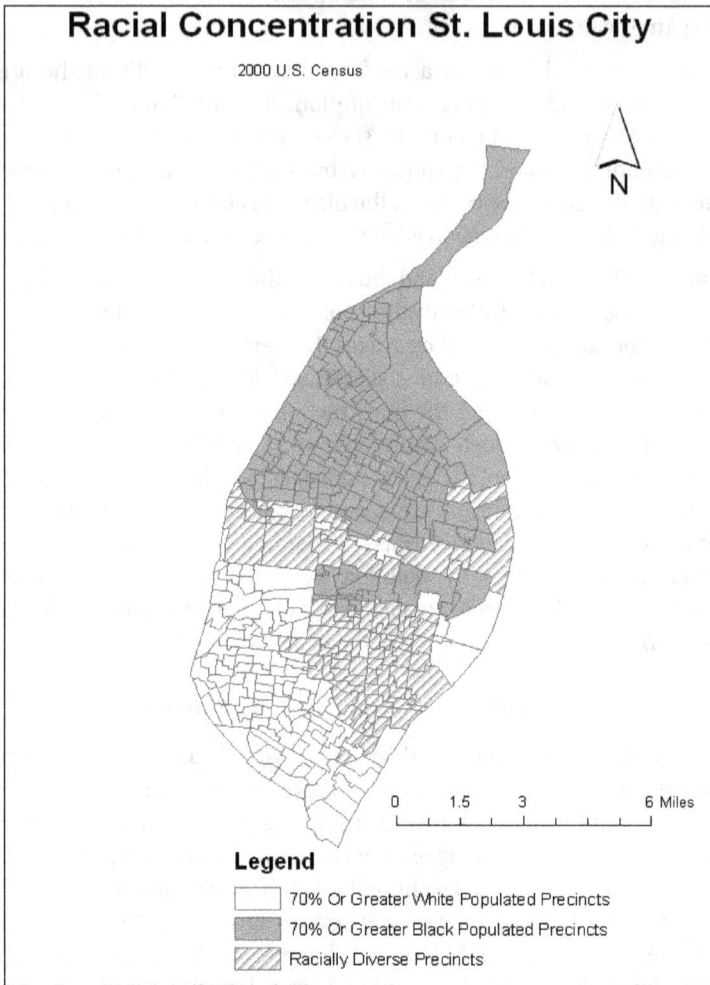

Racial Concentration St. Louis City

2000 U.S. Census

N

0   1.5   3   6 Miles

Legend

☐ 70% Or Greater White Populated Precincts

■ 70% Or Greater Black Populated Precincts

▨ Racially Diverse Precincts

70% Population % Defines Racial Identity of Precinct

Source: St. Louis City Government, GIS Department: Geospatial Research and GIS (stlouis-mo.gov).

The historical vestiges of American residential segregation are strong. African American residents of large urban cities were historically pigeonholed into segregated sections. Black residents in St. Louis at the turn of the twentieth century resided in the downtown or near downtown area. The area was surrounded by slaughterhouses, railroad lines, warehouses, and factories which combined to make it one of the least desirable areas for residential housing. Chicago's sectionalized segregation mirrored Saint Louis; recent immigrants inhabited concentric areas located in the downtown area, but gradually moved in waves beyond their initial areas of concentration (Warren, 1929). The black inhabitants were not allowed the assimilation gains of their white immigrant neighbors and, for most of the century, remained in the concentrated areas via racially restrictive real estate covenants or open discrimination (Stein, 2002).

Federal policy increased the rate of American home ownership while streamlining geographical segregation and suburbanization. The Federal Home Mortgage Agency (FHA) is a New Deal program established to channel credit to build and/or modernize single-family homes. The agency does not directly finance home loans. It insures the loans, providing a level of protection to lenders. It also streamlined the process of purchasing homes by popularizing the long-term amortized home mortgage and codifying appraisal and credit qualification guidelines.

The property appraisal guidelines sanctioned by the FHA helped to strengthen racial segregation. The FHA's official underwriting manual allowed private appraisals to systematically lower the appraisal value of property situated near African Americans, which pushed white property owners to sale property (that appraised lower) or not to buy at all (Kruse and Sugrue, 2005, p. 31).[2] The result was a mass exodus of whites from urban neighborhoods that were geographically close to blacks. Blacks were systematically denied loans by private lenders; the effect was a rise in home ownership by whites and increased renting of homes by blacks in concentrated urban core areas (Kruse and Sugrue, 2005, p. 31). The FHA appraisal guidelines valued single-family homes at higher rates then multi-family structures, which favored sprawling suburban areas over denser urban areas.[3] Finally, federal tax policy favors single-family suburban home ownership by offering substantial tax credits to homeowners.

A second form of geographical segregation involved local real estate covenants and local ordinances. Local ordinances were written that legally denied the sale of homes to blacks in designated areas or banks, realtors, and homeowners colluded not to sell homes in certain areas to black families. In 1916, St. Louis voters adapted a segregation ordinance forbidding the sale of

---

[2] The same guidelines were applied to Jewish Americans and other minorities.

[3] Returning World War II veterans increased single-family suburban home ownership with VA loans which mirrored the appraisal guidelines of the FHA. The Civil Rights Act of 1964 and Kennedy's 1962 executive order banning federal financing of segregated housing forced the end of race specific appraisal guidelines.

homes to African Americans in designated areas. The ordinance was found to be unconstitutional by the courts, but Stein (2002, p. 126) writes that the, "Restrictive covenants and realtor practices combined to carry out the intent of the ordinance..." [4] George Lipsitz (1988, p. 68) describes the segregated nature of St. Louis housing in the 1950s:

> In the 1950s the area of the city [St. Louis] open to black residents increased from 500 to 650 square blocks, but all 150 of these new blocks had already been designated as deteriorating or blighted by the City Plan Commission before blacks moved in. Loan agencies refused to extend credit to whites for purchases in those areas, further encouraging white flight. Unscrupulous realtors exploited the black demand for housing (as well as hostility to blacks) by "blockbusting"—frightening white homeowners about declining property values in order to panic them into selling houses at low prices that realtors could then resell to blacks at inflated prices.

The historical institutional rules of the mid-twentieth century were steeped in geographic segregation, but what if we examine the space of residency within the context of the present. Will we witness similar geographic outcomes? The answer is witnessed within *Map 6.1*, African American St. Louis residents reside in defined racial enclaves. Openly sanctioned government housing discrimination rules are unlawful, but minority home ownership is sharply narrowed by private institutional factors, redlining.

The term "redlining" originates from mid-century neighborhood maps that outlined restrictive areas of minority and nonminority residency. Within private appraisal and mortgage lending institutions, the practice continues. Often, areas with higher concentrations of minority population, have decreased home appraisal values. The outcomes are measurable with a clear gap in white to minority home ownership rates: 73 percent of white families own and occupy their homes; 47.5 percent of Latino Americans own and occupy their homes; 57.7 percent of Asian Americans own and occupy their homes; and 42.1 percent of African Americans own and occupy their homes (U.S. Census Bureau, 2019).

America is a mobile society with at least ten million Americans relocating from one American county to another each year (Beaudoin, 2013). The question arises how this relocation relates to "white flight." The simplest

---

[4] In 1948, the Supreme Court outlawed racially restrictive covenants in the case of *Shelley v. Kraemer*. The case emanated in St. Louis.

definition of "white flight" is the move of white city-dwellers to the suburbs to escape the influx of minorities. The definition is buttressed by the work of Kyle Crowder (2000, p. 223) who writes, ".... [T]he results indicate that the annual likelihood of leaving the neighborhood increases significantly with the size of the minority population in the neighborhood, and whites are especially likely to leave neighborhoods containing combinations of multiple minority groups."

There are alternate arguments buttressing the movement of whites to the suburbs after the conclusion of World War II. Kevin Kruse and Thomas Sugrue (2005) observed that many Americans moved from the inner cities simply because single-family homes were being built in the suburbs, the interstate highway system lessened commute times, and simple class mobility. Yet institutionally, during this wave of movement to the suburbs, minorities were systemically denied access to suburban homeownership opportunities by colluding banks and realtors through the "redlining" process. Leah Boustan (2010) further counters the non-race-based basis of "white flight" and argues that "white flight" was enhanced by an influx of African Americans from the South to the North.

Wellston, Missouri, is and has been a predominately African American suburb of St. Louis, Missouri for over fifty years. The tiny municipality has a population of just over 2,300 with more than 90 percent African American and a majority living at or below the poverty threshold (U.S. Census Bureau, 2010). A member of the burgeoning black middle-class and a key beneficiary of the Civil Rights Era longed to leave the racially homogenous small community in the late 1960s.

In 1968, Larman Williams was the African American assistant principle of the all-black Wellston High School. His wife was a special schoolteacher for the state of Missouri. During the summer of 1968, Mr. and Mrs. Williams sought to purchase a home in the nearby suburb of Ferguson to share with their three young daughters. In 1968, Ferguson's population was racially as homogenous as Wellston, only majority white, and initially, the real estate agent refused to display Mr. Williams' available homes. At the time, there was a small neighborhood in Ferguson comprised solely by poor African Americans. Mr. Williams subsequently made inquiries and learned that his potential white neighbors objected to the home being sold to an African American. After the intervention of a white clergyman, the white homeowners' fears were defused, and Mr. Williams became the first African American homeowner in Ferguson's middle-class neighborhoods.

Prior to the Williams purchase of their home in the predominantly white middle-class neighborhood, Mr. Williams once resided in the border suburb of Kinloch, Missouri. Like Wellston, Kinloch was and is predominantly black and impoverished. During the 1960s, Kinloch was literally cutoff from the then predominantly white Ferguson. Ferguson was a "sundown town" from which African Americans were banned after sundown with police harassment to follow brave blacks that challenged the policy, and the main road that connected Kinloch to Ferguson was blocked with a chain after dark; but a second road was kept open during the day for black day workers to enter and leave their jobs as nannies and maids.

The racial segregation stretched to education with the Kinloch and other tiny St. Louis County municipalities designated as members of Unincorporated St. Louis County until the 1930s. During the 1930s, politically the white-inhabited neighborhoods separated from Kinloch incorporating into the city of Berkley. The political move ensured that the schools would remain racially segregated with Kinloch schools remaining completely black with a shrinking tax base until the federal courts forced integration of the school systems during the mid-1970s.

Other African Americans followed the Williams family to Ferguson, but by 1970, only two years after their initial purchase, only 1 percent of the Ferguson population was African American. By 1980, Ferguson's African American population grew to 14 percent (U.S. Census Bureau, 1980). During the period, northern first ring suburbs boarding St. Louis were experiencing increases in African American population while south and western first ring St. Louis suburbs witnessed little increase in black population growth.

In 1990, Ferguson was mostly comprised of single-family one-story homes. The inhabitants of the homes were mostly working-class families, and racially the small municipality was roughly 67.4 percent white and 25 percent African American (U.S. Census Bureau, 1990). Yet twenty years later, the population of the small municipality was inversed with the white population dropping to 6,206 from 16,454 in 1990 (U.S. Census Bureau, 2010). One of many underlying sociopolitical variables leading to the change in population composition was public policy.

White flight took hold in the tiny suburban municipality over the twenty-year period, and increasingly the housing dynamics of the tiny municipality began to reflect the changes. In the 1990s, Ferguson was a municipality of majority single-family owner-occupied homes. As whites started to leave, the local government began to allow for the construction of low and mixed-income housing apartments. Investment firms bought out underwater mortgages and rented the homes to minorities. Overall, the practices in Ferguson mirror the housing practices of the nation.

Lenders and real estate agents still steer families to areas with populations of similar races, white families still flee areas with growing minority populations, and family and immigrant networks still attract groups of people similar to themselves. On a macro level community are racially heterogeneous, but on a neighborhood level, Americans reside in racially homogeneous communities. Neighborhoods become defined as "black," "white," "Asian," or "Latino."

This policy-centered segregation is fostered by policy choices. White suburban communities make policy decisions that keep minorities out. The use of exclusionary zoning laws, that outlaw the construction of mixed-use developments serves as an exclusionary tool to prevent the construction of mixed-income housing. Municipalities therefore compete for residents; banning apartment buildings or affordable housing that increases the likelihood of the municipality to attract affluent white taxpayers.

The unwillingness of white Americans to allow their children to be educated beside African Americans was witnessed by the reaction of whites to forced bussing programs in the late 1970s and early eighties in Boston, St. Louis, Kansas City, and New Jersey. The legal necessity to desegregate public education even witnessed legal action in 2016 when the Cleveland, Mississippi school board was forced to desegregate its predominantly segregated high school by the federal courts.

The Politics of the Racial Contract

Charles Mills (1997)' framework states that, "white supremacy should be thought of as itself a political system." The preceding historical outline illustrates the presence of historical institutional barriers in both the growth of minority home ownership and the place where minorities reside. V.O. Key (1949) examination of the American sociopolitical system during the period preceding the economic decline of the Great Depression was a country that reinforced the lower caste status of African Americans. The politics of the post-Civil War South was dominated by one political party, the Democratic Party. For post-Civil War Southerners, the Republican Party was the political party of Scalawags and freed African Americans. From the period of the official ending of the Reconstruction, the American South was dominated by the Democratic Party. Between the years 1875 to 1965, no Republican-held statewide or federal offices for the states of Louisiana, Mississippi, or Alabama. V.O. Key's (1949) seminal study of post-World War II Southern society highlighted a white populace that competed for socioeconomic resources with African Americans. He found that whites residing near blacks exhibited negative contextual responses to African Americans—the "black threat" hypothesis and a friend's and neighbor's effect took place for electoral decisions.

Key found that as one traveled northbound from the "deep" South that the population density of African Americans decreased and, with it, partisan support for the Democratic Party. What this meant politically, was there was relatively little difference between the policy prescriptions of opposing white Southern politicians. It was a political environment that political scientists refer to as low salience, and elections were decided during the Republican primary elections. This created an effect observed by Richard Fenno (1977) in which he observed for congressional elections incumbent candidates navigated three interwoven geographies of election constituencies, the most important, the personal vote. A term to describe the very intimate and base supporters of candidates, "In some cases they are his closest political advisors and confidants. In other cases, they are people from whom he draws emotional sustenance for his political work" (Fenno, 1977, p. 889). A large proportion of the incumbency advantage owes to the personal vote, as opposed to the quality of the challenger and ideological party cues given to voters.[5]

The beginning of World War II witnessed the first organized angst against America's race-based social order by middle-class African Americans. It was witnessed with the threat of organized protest as America increasingly ramped up its industrial and social gears for war. The political challenges to the social order were signified by seminal calls from a then-burgeoning politician from Minneapolis, Hubert Humphrey. His call to add a civil rights plank to the 1948 Democratic Party's convention, resulted in the first cracks to the New Deal coalition.

Southern white Dixiecrats were willing to fracture their successful New Deal Coalition with the hint of guarantying basic rights to African Americans, as witnessed by Strom Thurmond's 1948 third-party candidacy for president. Guaranteeing equal rights to African Americans challenged an entrenched social order (the racial contract) that perched whites at its apex. Yet the two decades after the ending of World War II would witness a mobilization of the African American middle-class to cement a challenge to America's social order. The fight would follow the practices of the previous century in which the judicial branch was utilized as a tool to codify the racial order. African Americas legally challenged the stalwart of segregation in the highest court, the separate but equal doctrine and won. Coupled with early concessions from the executive branch, the desegregation of the armed forces, the ten years between 1955-1965

---

[5] The quality of the challenger owes to the intuition that incumbents may win because they are the best candidates running, and they do noticeably worse when they face state legislators and other experienced challengers.

were the most substantial years of civil rights expansion since the ending of the civil war, a hundred years before, but these political strides were catalyst for the political mobilization of Southern Democrats.

In a preceding chapter, the political migration of Southern Democrats to the Republican Party was highlighted. It was a movement less based on ideological difference, but in an adherence to the racial contract. American individual political perceptions have historically been filtered through race-based lenses. W.E.B. Du Bois (1903) described a raced based consciousness for African Americans. The same holds for America's whites; that policy prescriptions are filtered through these lenses, with the help of elites to define the issue as pro-minority, neutral, or anti-minority. Political scientists argue that most issues require a requisite knowledge that most Americans do not possess, and people turn to sociopolitical elites to define the issues (Zaller, 1992). For most Americans, these elites are politicians, journalist, or contextually in this age of social networking, someone commenting via the internet.

The adherence to race-based consciousness played out within the aftermath of the 2020 general election. The Democratic Party's commitment to civil rights witnessed the migration of Southern Democrats to the Republican Party during the last decades of the twentieth century. This movement was solidified in the American South, the former states of the confederacy. The movement solidified within the state of Georgia, a state preceding the 2020 general election that was solidly represented at the state and federal level by white Republican office holders. Yet the political environment was slowly disturbed be demographic changes. Georgia's population is 57.8 percent white, 31.9 percent African American, and 4.1 percent Asian (U.S. Census Bureau, 2021). If we were to look at a map of Georgia, we would notice that the African American population is concentrated within key population centers (Fulton County, Cobb County, and Gwinnett County) and this explains the high percentage of Georgia minority local and state office holders, 135, but prior to the 2020 election, Georgia lacked a post-reconstruction era minority United States Senator, Governor, Lieutenant Governor, or any other significant statewide officeholders. In fact, Georgia's statewide and federal offices were dominated by white members of the Republican Party, but Georgia's African American population was solidly aligned with the Democratic Party.

The demographic changes played out during the 2020 general election. The election witnessed high voter turnout in the most populous Georgia counties of Fulton, Cobb, and Gwinnett. The high voter turnout in the counties was correlated to increased levels of African American voter turnout. The high population Georgia county voters heavily supported Democratic Party candidates. The result was the election of the first post-reconstruction era

African American Georgia Senator, Raphael Warnock, a second Democratic Senator, John Ossoff, and the Democratic presidential candidate taking the state's electoral college votes. The immediate result of the election by the majority lead Republican Georgia legislature was the passage of voter restriction laws, which would broadly affect African American voters. Restrictive voting laws that harken back to the "Jim Crow" era: "the laws limit the use of ballot drop boxes, narrows the time frame voters have to request and return mail-in ballots, imposes strict identification requirements, and prohibits election officials from sending unsolicited ballot application to voters."

The Social Basis of Proximity and the Racial Contract

The racial threat hypothesis or the racial contract plays out in the geography of criminal justice. During the summers of 2012- 2019, incidents in Minnesota, Missouri, Florida, Louisiana, and New York witnessed the death of several African American men after encounters with law enforcement. The purpose of this section is not to litigate the illegality or the morality of the encounters; the purpose is to examine the often race-based public sentiment to the responses, which must be placed within the scope of the racial contract. During the summer of 2014, widespread riots erupted in Ferguson, Missouri after it was announced that charges would not be sought against the police officer involved in the encounter that resulted in the death of African American Michael Brown. A widespread mantra directed at protestors, was that African Americans should focus on the crime that riddles inner-city communities.

The fact is that the leading cause of death of young African American men is gunfire, and that the gunfire is statistically more likely to come from the hands of other African American men cannot and should not be disputed; however, the desire to be treated fairly and legally by government officials cannot be equated with criminal activity. It is simply an ad hominem fallacy, which simply means attacking the person instead of the argument. The two things are not the same, and social scientists have observed that crime is geographic (Weisburd et al., 2006; Wilson et al., 2009; and Hipp et al., 2004). Supporting the geographic nature of crime is the racially homogenous nature of American neighborhoods (Brady, 2006; Jackson, 1985; Massey, 1987; Siskind, 2005), and the simplest of crime control theory, which holds that for a crime to occur, the following factors must be available: a willing assailant, a potential victim, and the lack of a guardian (police officer) to prevent the crime (Gottfredson, 2006, p. 77).

Basically, in geographically racially homogenous neighborhoods, crimes are committed and perpetuated statistically more often by members of the homogenous racial group. This is presented in nationally reported crime data: 83.5 percent of crimes perpetrated against whites are committed by other whites; 90 percent of crimes perpetrated against African Americans are perpetrated by other African Americans, although whites are 83 percent more likely to be the perpetrators when the victim is Latino/Hispanic (Federal Bureau of Investigation, 2013).[6]

One cannot simply focus on crime without examining disparities in the legal system. The constitution affords all citizens the right to a jury trial composed of their peers, but for African Americans, this is often problematic with 39 percent of African American jurors being excluded before trial while only 19 percent of other races are excluded (O'Brian and Grosso, 2012). The practice was forbidden by the 1986 Supreme Court ru ing in *Batson v. Kentucky*, <u>476 U.S. 79</u> (1986), and reaffirmed in 2016 in *Foster v. Chatman.*

Two other facts about African American interactions with the legal system include disparities in bail and plea deals. Often overworked public defenders advise clients to accept plea deals that often include a percentage of jail time possible with conviction or simply probation, but African Americans have a 23 percent greater chance of jail time included in plea deals than whites (Vera Institute of Justice, 2015). African Americans are more likely to be jailed while awaiting trial than white defendants with 59 percent of black defendants awaiting trial in jail, while 41 percent of whites are released via bond or their own recognizance (Vera Institute of Justice, 2015).

During the late 1960s and early 1970s, a heroin epidemic ravaged major urban areas. The heroin epidemic slowed by the early 1990s with an estimated 500,000 heroin users residing in the United States by 1992. Former New York State Division of Substance Abuse Services Chief of Epidemiology explained to the New York Times in 1992, "I'm sure that AIDS has neutralized the demand for heroin. And crack has dominated the drug scene, giving users something to" (New York Times, September 13th, 1989).

The upsurge in crack cocaine use would spur a famous response from then-President George H.W. Bush. On September 5th, 1989, President Bush spoke from the Oval Office and declared a law enforcement-based "War on Drugs." President Bush highlighted his speech by holding a bag of crack cocaine to highlight the focus of the law enforcement efforts. It set the tone of a zero-tolerance drug policy and criminalized not only the distribution of crack cocaine but the simple possession of the narcotic. Possessing the powdered

---

[6] It should be noted that the data is self-reported, and many Latinos and Hispanics personally identify as white, which may skew the data.

form of the narcotic did not carry the same punishment as possessing the crack form of the narcotic, and as a result, America witnessed an increasing number of arrests for drug-related offenses.

During the decade between 2000-2010, America's drug epidemic flipped from the poor inner cities to the affluent and predominantly white suburbs. From 2002-2013, there was a 114 percent increase in white users of heroin and a 63 percent increase in drug users with incomes of $50,000 or more (CDC, 2016). In 2000, African Americans between the ages of 45-64 held the highest death rate for overdosing on heroin, but by 2015, whites between the ages of 18-44 had the highest rate of overdosing on heroin (CDC, 2016.) In fact, non-white users of heroin have decreased (CDC, 2016).

In recent years, the heroin issue was coined an epidemic, a word synonymous with health. The term epidemic is defined as a widespread occurrence of an infectious disease in a community at a particular time. In February 2016, the Republican-led congress passed a drug treatment-and-prevention bill sponsored by conservative Republican Senator Rob Portman, the legislation was specifically designed to address heroin usage and users. Senator Portman remarked after the passage of the bill, "This is for real," Portman told Ohio reporters after the committee vote. "This will make a difference in the lives of the people who I represent." The average increase in heroin use and the growing percentages of white heroin users can be viewed in *Table 6.1.*

Table 6.1: Annual average rate of heroin use (per 1,000 people in each group)

	2002–2004*	2011–2013*	Percent Change
Sex			
Male	2.4	3.6	50%
Female	0.8	1.6	100%
Age, Years			
12–17	1.8	1.6	--
18–25	3.5	7.3	109%
26 or older	1.2	1.9	58%
Race / Ethnicity			
Non-Hispanic white	1.4	3	114%
Other	2	1.7	--
Annual Household Income			
Less than $20,000	3.4	5.5	62%
$20,000–$49,999	1.3	2.3	77%
$50,000 or more	1	1.6	60%

Source: Centers for Disease Control and Prevention. 2016. https://www.cdc.gov/drug overdose/data/heroin.html

Michael Botticelli, the Obama White House Director of National Drug Control Policy, commented on the difference between the parents of heroin addicts as opposed to crack cocaine addicts,

> Because the demographic of people affected are more white, more middle class, these are parents who are empowered, and… [T]hey know how to call a legislator, they know how to get angry with their insurance company, they know how to advocate. They have been so instrumental in changing the conversation. (Seelye, 2015)

Katherine Seelye (2015) writes the following about the parents of heroin addicts and the overall political response to the growing problem of heroin addiction:

> Their [the parents of heroin addicts] efforts also include lobbying statehouses, holding rallies and starting nonprofit organizations, making these mothers and fathers part of a growing backlash against the harsh tactics of traditional drug enforcement. These days, in rare bipartisan or even nonpartisan agreement, punishment is out and compassion is in.

The issue is that when the drug of choice was crack cocaine and the users were poor urban-based minorities, the public response was zero tolerance, incarceration, and lengthy prison sentences. However, the response is different when the drug users are not predominantly poor citizens residing away from the emerald-green manicured lawns of suburbia. It is a health crisis, not a law enforcement crisis, which plays to the racial lenses of the racial contract; white privilege dictates the framing and the policy choices regarding the codification and response to public problem definition.

Conclusion

The racial contract relies on the imagined social construct of race materialized as skin color or pigmentation differences. The American white working class is inundated by elite appeals casting the socioeconomic struggle as a two-variable game or a zero-sum choice (Zaller, 1992). It defines, non-white status as outside the benefits of the social contract. Policies or collective socioeconomic actions that are cast as beneficial to the "other" are rejected, with the zero-sum calculus—that any potential benefit awarded to the other potentially disrupts the social order, the racial contract.

The political framing of the racial contract is weaponized in veiled political appeals. Lee Atwater served as a key campaign strategist of the 1988 George H.W. Bush presidential campaign.

> You start out in 1954 saying "Nigger, nigger, nigger." By 1968 you can't say "nigger"—that hurts you. Backfires. So you say stuff like forced busing, states' rights, and all that stuff. You're getting so abstract no [that] you're talking about cutting taxes, and all these things you're re-talking about are totally economic things and a by-product of them is [that] blacks get hurt worse than whites. And subconsciously maybe that is part of it. "I'm not saying that. But I'm saying that if it is getting that abstract, and that coded, that we are doing away with the racial problem one way or the other. You follow me—because obviously sitting around saying, "we want to cut this" is much more abstract than even the busing thing and a hell of a lot more abstract than "Nigger, nigger" (Lamis, 1999, p. 8).

Atwater's words ring true to a racially charged strategy with the primary goal of appealing to the racist's views of a section of the American electorate and electorate that is bifurcated by both race and space.

Postscript

"It is acknowledged, namely, that there are in the world three forms of government, autocracy, oligarchy, and democracy: autocracies and oligarchies are administered according to the tempers of their lords, but democratic states according to established laws."

Aeschines

The study utilized the United States as the unit of analysis, but the framework is universal within an interconnected world economic system. During the second decade of the twenty-first century, the Western world grabbles with liberalism, and appears to be open to illiberalism. Totalitarian regimes in Hungary, Poland, Brazil, Russia, Turkey, and the Philippines have witnessed the rise of regimes that openly bemoan the loss of the imagined nationalism, with vibrant appeals to the imagined past impeded within the communal contract (Applebaum, 2020). In Poland, the Law and Justice Party, Prawo i Sprawiedliwość, openly scapegoats Syrian immigrants as the other and the imagined pollutant to civil society, although Syrian immigration is minimal. It also has retooled an antisemitic past with outright propaganda bemoaning the imagined interference of Jewish elites in societal decay.

The American and British right have become the trumpeters of white nationalism, openly embracing xenophobia, and white anger. The triumph of the second World War was the defeat of fascism, and the triumph of the Cold War was the defeat of communism. It was the triumph of liberalism, but illiberalism, with its rejection of independent government institutions, such as independent judiciaries and independent media are on the rise, as tools to extend imagined nationalistic identities. It is a rejection of diversity for, not so veiled, appeals of imagined uniformity. The dynamic social contract offers a framework to explore these dynamic regressions of the Western social contract.

The regression of the imagined community was witnessed by clear xenophobic appeals of the pro-Brexit British United Kingdom Independence Party and its leader Nigel Farage. The political party openly campaigned for the British referendum to exit the European Union, arguing that British membership within the body amounted to a loss of sovereignty; although, the British were the key architects of the single European market. During the weeks before the Brexit vote, UKIP ran anti-Syrian and Turkish political ads, which portrayed Turkish acceptance into the European Union, with images of "brown" people overwhelming British hospitals and social welfare programs, and hordes of Syrian refugees in route to the British border. In reality, the United Kingdom was never part of the Shengen Area, the areas freely accepting Syrian civil war refugees, and the United Kingdom was never obligated to support Turkish entry into the European Union. The appeals were openly xenophobic and far within the context of the racial contract. The appeals were based on imagined historical nostalgia for the distant past in which membership within the social contract were clearly defined by skin color, ethnic identity, language, or outright nationalism (Applebaum, 2021).

Applebaum (2021) and Stenner (2005) equally explore the appeal of autocracy within a similar context, which can be simplified as the dynamic social contract.

> ...that the 'authoritarian predisposition' ...It is better described as simple-mindness: people are often attracted to authoritarian ideas because they are bothered by complexity. They dislike divisiveness. They prefer unity. A sudden onslaught of diversity—diversity of opinions, diversity of experiences... (Applebaum, 2021, p. 106).

The researchers are dually alluding to the constrained and dynamic nature of the Western social contract. It is exclusive, it rejects diversity for the imagined communal past, and is dynamic within its open contraction. The question becomes what is the impetus for the reaction and the contraction of the Western social contract. The answer lies within the Western political and socioeconomic institutions. Institutions that are the dual result of the triumph of liberalism and international capitalism.

The conflict of the twentieth century was ideological and centered on two ideologies that both originate from enlightenment theory, Wilsonian liberalism and Leninist Marxism (Wallerstein, 2004). The conflict was unfair, as capitalism had a four-hundred-year advantage. Fascism briefly reared its head in the aftermath of the world's decades-long economic depression, but for most of the century, the battle lines were clearly defined. At the conclusion of the twentieth century, there was a clear winner, Wilsonian liberalism.

The Wilsonian-liberal institutions triumphed with the collapse of the Soviet Union. The world economic system completely reorganized within the confides of the liberal creed and the American post-war Bretton Woods's stalwart institutions. Former Warsaw Pack nations embraced liberalism and fortified protection from their former ideological overlord, the Soviets, by joining the post-war alliance embodied by the North Atlantic Treaty Organization: Estonia, Latvia, Lithuania, Bulgaria, Romania, Slovakia, Hungary, Poland, and Slovenia.

Even China, embraced the world economic order, but not the sociopolitical institutions.

The conflict within Western nations is no longer ideological; it is tribal and centered within the imagined past (Applebaum, 2020). An "imagined past" that harkens back to the inner geographies of the dynamic social contract. The French National Front Party embodies this dynamic retraction of the social contract with its unrestrained appeals to the racial contract and the dynamic rejection of global interconnectedness.

Western Europe of the nineteenth and early twentieth centuries was a continent of emigration, but post-war Europe witnessed mass immigration. Waves of immigrants that were the by-product of labor demands for a rebuilding a war-ravaged continent. In France, prior to World War I, the movement of labor followed the same trends witnessed in the United States. Rural French citizens and immigrants migrated to the growing industrial areas of Northern and Eastern France. However, the foreign workers who joined the French migration to the industrializing urban centers were predominately Belgian and Italian (Deley, 1983, p. 197).

The devastation of the post-World War II France witnessed a different pattern of immigration. By 1971, the demand for French labor peaked with 3.4 million foreign-born workers. Most of the foreign-born French workers immigrated from North Africa: Algeria, Morocco, and Tunisia. The apex of French immigration coincided with the ending of the post-war economic boom, and by 1974 the French government had effectively closed borderless immigration.

The 1970s economic decline can be associated with a global rise in fuel prices, but can include the variable of capital wage substitution, globalization. Industrial-based technological increases deflated production costs. Simply, the tools and machinery of production became less costly than labor. The differential changes increased the mobility of capital, as factory retooling and relocation became less costly than labor, with labor or wages remaining static or declining. Empirically, real unit French labor cost remained static over the period 1970 to 1986, with an average of 100 while French unemployment doubled: 1973 (2.7 percent unemployment); 1979 (5.9 percent unemployment), and 1987 (10.5 percent unemployment) (Lombard, 1984, p. 54). This highlights the economic shift that enveloped the world beginning in the 1970s, in which production and capital began to freely cross international borders.

The French response was heightened appeals to the racial contract with a dual appeal for a broader dynamic retraction of the social contract. The most vocal of the appeals originated from a former populist, anti-communist, and veteran of the French Foreign Legion, Jean Louis Le Pen. In 1972, Le Pen organized the Front National Party and in 1974 rode its banner for a run for the French presidency. Le Pen garnered less than one percent of the vote, following a campaign in which he openly railed against North African immigrants and French membership within international institutions. In 2011, Le Pen was succeeded in the leadership of the National Front by his daughter, Marine Le Pen. The National Front Party of the younger Le Pen continued anti-immigrant, anti-sematic, and anti-globalized rhetoric, and during the 2017 French presidential campaign Marine Le Pen made the following statement,

> Immigration is an organized replacement of our population. This threatens our very survival. We don't have the means to integrate those who are already here. The result is endless cultural conflict (Mesoudi, 2018).

Marine Le Pen was able to garner 33.9 percent of the French vote.

The French National Front Party has not successfully won the reigns of power, but the strategy has won electoral success in America, Poland, Turkey, Brazil, and the Philippines. Again, it is not an ideological fight. It is closer to populism, and it relies on economic and social disaffection to be met with outright appeals to the racial contract for the imagined past, nationalism.

References

Anderson, B. (1983). *Imagined Communities Reflections on the Origin and Spread of Nationalism*. New York: Verso.

Applebaum, A. (2020). *Twilight of Democracy the Seductive Lure of Authoritarianism*. New York: Anchor Books.

Appleby, J. (2010). *Relentless Revolution A History of Capitalism*. New York: W.W. Norton & Company, Inc.

Baptist, E. (2001). "Cuffy," "Fancy Maids," and "One-Eyed Men": Rape, Commodification, and the Domestic Slave Trade in the United States. *The American Historical Review*, 106(5), 1619-1650.

Bartley, T., Bergesen, A., Boswell, T., Chase, D., & Dunaway, W. (2000). *A World-Systems Reader: New Perspectives on Gender, Urbanism, Cultures, Indigenous Peoples, and Ecology 1st Edition*. New York: Rowman & Littlefield Publishers, Inc.

Baybeck, B. (2006). "Sorting Out the Competing Effects of Racial Context." *The Journal of Politics* 68(2): 386-396.

Beaudoin, J. (2013). "Net Migration Patterns for U.S. Counties," *The Applied Population Laboratory at the University of Wisconsin- Madison*. Retrieved on September 17, 2016 from Madison, University of Wisconsin: http://www.net migration.wisc.edu/ Beck, U. (1997). *Was ist Globalisierung? Irrtumer des Globalismus-Antworten auf Globalisierung*. Frankfurt: Suhrkamp.

Beckert, S. (2014). *Empire of Cotton A Global History*. New York: Alfred A. Knopf.

Beer, S. (2006). *Encounters with Modernity*. In R. Rhodes, S. Binder, & B. Rockman, The Oxford Handbook of Political Institutions (pp. 693-715). New York: Oxford University Press.

Bentley, A. (1949). *The Process of Government*. Evanston: Principia Press.

Boustan, L. (2010). "Was Postwar Suburbanization 'White Flight'? Evidence from the Black Migration," *The Quarterly Journal of Economics*, 125(1): 417-443.

Breitzer, S. R. (2011). Race, Immigration, and Contested Americanness: Black Nativism and the American Labor Movement, 1880-1930. *Reworking Race and Labor*, 4(2), 269-283.

Bridges, A. (1984). *A City in the Republic*. Cambridge, U.K.: Cambridge University Press.

Bryce, J. (1929). *Modern Democracies*. London: McMillan.

Buckley, W., & Passos, J. (1959). *Up from Liberalism*. New York: McDowell, Obolensky.

Campbell, A., Converse, P. E., Miller, W. E., & Stokes, D. (1960). *The American Voter*. New York: Wiley.

Chait, J. (2021, September 16). The National Interest. Retrieved February 22, 2022, from *Intelligencer*: https://nymag.com/intelligencer/article/fact-check-richest-1-dont-pay-40-of-the-taxes.html

Chamberlain, A. (2006). *Demography in Archaeology*. Cambridge: Cambridge University Press.

Chilcote, R. (2002). Globalization or Imperialism? *Latin American Perspectives*, 29(6), 80-84.

Clabaugh, G. (2004). The Cutting Edge the Educational Legacy of Ronald Reagan. *Educational Horizons*, 256-259.

Conlan, T. (1998). *From New Federalism to Devolution Twenty-Five Years of Intergovernmental Reform*. Washington D.C.: Brookings Institution Press.

Control, C. O. (1999). MMWR. Retrieved from CDC U.S. Government: Retrieved June 22, 2022, from: https://www.cdc.gov/mmwr/preview/mmwr html/mm4829a1.htm

Crowder, K. (2000). "The racial context of white mobility: An individual-level assessment of the white flight hypothesis." *Social Science Research*, 29(2): 223-257.

Dahl, R. (2003). *How Democratic is the American Constitution? Second Edition*. New Haven: Yale University Press.

Dark, T. E. (1996). Organized Labor and Congressional Democrats: Reconsidering the 1980s. *Political Science Quarterly*, 111(1): 83-104.

Dator, J. A., Pratt, R., & So, Y. (2006). *What is Globalization?* In J. A. Dator, Fairness, Globalization, and Public Institutions (pp. 13-18). Honolulu: University of Hawai'i Press.

Deley, M. (1981). "French Immigration Policy Since May 1981," *The International Migration Review*, 17(2): 196-211.

Douglas, P. H. (1968). *American Apprenticeship and Industrial Education*. New York: Columbia University Press.

Dray, P. (2010). *There Is Power in A Union: The Epic Story of Labor in America*. New York: Double Day.

Du Bois, W. (1918, February). "The Black Man and the Unions." Retrieved February 26, 2022, from Teaching American History: https://teachingamericanhistory.org/document/the-black-man-and-the-unions/

Fauntroy, M. K. (2007). *Republicans and the Black Vote*, Boulder: Lynne Reiner Publishers, Inc.

Federal Bureau of Investigation. (2013). Uniform Crime Reports, Retrieved March 1st, 2022, from: https://www.fbi.gov/about-us/cjis/ucr/crime-in-the.u.s/2013/crime-in-the-u.s.-2013/offenses-known-to-law-enforcement/expanded-homicide/expanded_homicide_data_table_6_murder_race_and_sex_of_vicitm_by_race_and_sex_of_offender_2013.xls accessed April 7th, 2016.

Feldmeyer, B. (2018). *The Classical Assimilation Model a Controversial Canon*. In Routledge Handbook on Immigration and Crime. Routledge.

Fenno, R. (1977). "U.S. House Members in Their Constituencies." *American Political Science Review*, 71(3): 883-917.

Fergus, D. (2014, September 2). My students pay too much for college. Blame Reagan. *The Washington Post*. Retrieved July 9, 2021, from https://www.washingtonpost.com/posteverything/wp/2014/09/02/my-students-pay-too-much-for-college-blame-reagan/

Field, A. J. (2006). Technological Change and U.S. Productivity Growth in the Interwar Years. *The Journal of Economic History*, 66(1): 203-236.

Flint, C., & Taylor, P. (2011). *Political Geography World-economy, nation-state, and locality Sixth Edition*. Essex: Pearson.

Foner, P. (1975). *History of the Labor Movement in the United States Vol.2 From the Founding of the A.F. of L. to the Emergence of American Imperialism*. New York: International Publishers.

Foner, P. S., Sims, W., Williams, G. H., McCormack, A., Mehurin, C., Mattox, M., & Scott, B. (1968). The Knights of Labor. *The Journal of Negro History*, 53(1): 70-77.

Foner, P., & Lewis, R. (1980). *The Black Worker, Volume 5: The Black Worker from 1900 to 1919*. Philadelphia: Temple University Press.

Frank, T. (2004). *What's the Matter with Kansas? How Conservatives Won the Heart of America*. London: McMillan.

Friedman, T. (2005). *The World is Flat a Brief History of the Twenty-First Century*. New York: Farrar, Straus and Giroux.

Frymer, P. (2003). Acting When Elected Officials Won't: Federal Courts and Civil Rights Enforcement in U.S. Labor Unions, 1935-85. *The American Political Science Review*, 97(3): 483-499.

Fukuyama, F. (2014). *Political Order and Political Decay from the Industrial Revolution to the Globalization of Democracy*. New York: Farrar, Straus and Giroux.

Geisst, C. (2013). *Beggar Thy Neighbor: A History of Usury and Debt*. Philadelphia: University of Pennsylvania.

Glenn, E. N. (2002). *Unequal freedom: How race and gender shaped American citizenship and labor*. Cambridge: Harvard University Press.

Goldwater, B. (1960). *The Conscience of a Conservative*. Princeton: Princeton University Press.

Gourevitch, P. (1986). *Politics in Hard Times Comparative Responses to International Economic Crises*. Ithaca: Cornell University Press.

Gottfredson, M. (2006). "The Empirical Status of Control Theory in Criminology." In *Taking Stock The Status of Criminological Theory Advances in Criminological Theory Volume 15*, by Francis Cullen, John Paul Wright, and Kristie Blevins, 77-100, New Brunswick: Transaction Publishers.

Hamilton, A., Madison, J., Rossiter, C., Jay, J., & Kesler, C. R. (2005). *The federalist papers*. New York: Signet Classics.

Hanson-Jones, A. (1984). Wealth and Growth of the Thirteen Colonies: Some Implications. *The Journal of Economic History*, 44(2): 239-254.

Hardin, R. (1971). Collective Action as an agreeable n-prisoners' dilemma. *Systems Research and Behavioral Science*, 16: 472-81.

Hardin, R. (1968). The Tragedy of the Commons. *Science*, 162: 1243-1248.

Hartz, L. (1955). *The Liberal Tradition in America*. New York: Harcourt.

Henretta, J. A., Edwards, R., & Self, R. O. (2010). *America's History, Combined Volume*. Bedford: St. Martin's Press.

Hobbes, T., & MacPherson, C. (1651; 1981). *Leviathan*. New York: Penguin.

Isaac, L., McDonald, S., & Lukasic, G. (2006). Takin' It from the Streets: How the Sixties Mass Movement Revitalized Unionization. *American Journal of Sociology*, 112(1): 46-96.

Jackson, K. (1985). *Crabgrass Frontier The Suburbanization of the United States*. New York: Oxford University Press.

Jenkins, J. G., & Perrow, C. (1977). Insurgency of the Powerless: The Farm Worker Movements (1946-1972). *American Sociological Review*, 42(2): 249-265.

Johnson, N. (1975). The place of institutions in the study of politics. *Political Studies*, 25: 271-83.

Jordan, W. P. (1961). The Influence of the West Indies on the Origins of New England Slavery. *The William and Mary Quarterly*, 18(2): 243-250.

Judd, D., & Swanstrom, T. (2006). *City Politics: The Political Economy of Urban America 8th Edition*. St. Louis: Longman.

Kessler, S. H. (1952). The Organization of Negroes in the Knights of Labor. *The Journal of Negro History*, 37(3): 248-276.

Key, V. J. (1949). *Southern Politics in State and Nation*. New York: Alfred. A. Knopf.

Key, V. J. (1955). A Theory of Critical Elections. *Journal of Politics*, 17: 1-18.

Kingdon, J. (1984). Agendas, Alternatives, and Public Policy. New York: Pearson.

Kruse, K. and Sugrue, J. (2005). *The New Surburban History*. Chicago: The Univeristy of Chicago Press.

Lamis, A. (1999). "The Two-Party South: From the 1960s to the 1990s," In *Southern Politics in the 1990s*, by Alexander Lamis. Baton Rouge: Louisiana State University Press.

Lawson, S. (1991). *Running for Freedom: Civil Rights and Black Politics in America Since 1945*. Philadelphia: Temple University Press.

Lee, S. (2011). Immigration and Citizenship in Japan. *Social Science Japan Journal*, 14(1): 108-111.

Levitt, T. (1983). The Globalization of Markets. *Harvard Business Review*, 61(3): 92-102.

Lipsitz, G. (1988). *A Life in the Struggle: Ivory Perry and the Culture of Opposition*. Philadelphia: Temple University Press.

Locke, J. (1687; 2017). *Second Treatise of Government*. New York: Digireads Publishing.

Lombard, M. (1984). Analyzing the persistence of unemployment: The French experience. *International Contributions to Labour Studies*, 4: 53-72.

Lowenstein, R. (1995). Federal Grants During the Eighties. New York: Federal Reserve Bank of New York. Retrieved July 9, 2021, from https://www.newyork fed.org/medialibrary/media/research/staff_reports/research_papers/9508. pdf

Lowi, T. (1969). *The End of Liberalism Ideology, Policy, and the Crisis of Public Authority*. New York: Norton.

Mabbett, I.W. (1977). Varnas in Angkor and the Indian Caste System, *The Journal of Asian Studies*, 36(3): 429-442.

Massey, D., and Denton N. (1987). Trends in the Residential Segregation of Blacks, Hispanics, and Asians: 1970-1980, *American Sociological Review*, 52(6): 802-825.

Marino, J. A. (1993). Creative accounting in the age of Philip II? Determining the 'just' rate of interest. *The Historical Journal*, 36(04), 761-783.

Marx, K. (1867). *Das Kapital*. Germany: Verlag von Otto Meisner.

Marx, K., & Engels, F. (1958). *Selected Works in Two Volumes*. Robinson: Language Publishing House.

McRae, D. J., & Meldrum, J. A. (1960). Critical Elections in Illinois:1888-1958. *American Political Science Review*, 54: 669-685.

Mesoudi, A. (2018). Migration, acculturation, and the maintenance of between-group cultural variation. *PLoS One, 13*(10).

Mills, C. (1997). *The Racial Contract*. Ithaca: Cornell University Press.

Milojevic, I. (2006). A Critique of Globalization: Not Just a White Man's World. In J. Dator, D. Pratt, & Y. Seo, Fairness, *Globalization, and Public Institutions: East Asia and Beyond* (pp. 75-87). Honolulu: University of Hawaii Press.

Minor, J. (2008). Segregation Residual in Higher Education: A Tale of Two States. *American Educational Research Journal*, 45(4): 861-885.

Moehlman, A. (1934). The Christianization of Interest. Church History: 3(4): 3-15.

Morris, R. B. (1983). The Emergence of the American Labor. In R. B. Morris, *A History of the American Worker* (pp. 10-25). Princeton: Princeton University Press.

NBC News. (2015). http://www.nbcphiladelphia.com/news/local/Pool-Boots-Kids-Who-Might-Change-the-Complexion.html accessed 06/02/2015.

Nicholson, P. (1990). *The Political Philosophy of British Idealist: Selected Studies*. Cambridge: Cambridge University Press.

Niebuhr, R. (1932). *Moral Man and Immoral Society: A Study in Ethics and Politics*. Louisville: Westminster, John Knox Press.

North, D. (1990). *Institutions, Institutional Change and Economic Performance*. New York: Cambridge University Press.

O'Brian, B. and Grosso, M. (2012). A Stubborn Legacy: The Overwhelming Importance of Race in Jury Selection in 173 Post-Batson North Carolina Capitol Trials, 97 Iowa L. Rev. 1531.

Ostrom, E. (1990). *Governing the Commons The Evolution of Institutions for Collective Action*. Cambridge: Cambridge University Press.

Park, R. E. (1925). *The City*. Chicago: University of Chicago Press.

Parker, L., & Lynn, M. (2002). What's Race Got to Do with It? Critical Race Theory Conflicts with and Connection to Qualitative Research Methodology and Epistemologies. *Qualitative Inquiry*, 8(1): 7-22.

Pateman, C. (1988). *The Sexual Contract*. Stanford: Stanford University Press.

Pateman, C., & Mills, C. (2007). *Contract and Domination*. Cambridge: Polity Press.

Pautz, H. (2005). The politics of identity in Germany: The Leitkultur debate. *Race & Class*, 46(4): 39-52.

Phillips, K. (2002). *Wealth and Democracy a Political History of the American Rich*. New York: Broadway Books.

Piketty, T. (2003). Income Inequality in the United States, 1913-1998. *The Quarterly Journal of Economics*, 118(1): 1-39.

Piketty, T. (2015). About "Capital in the Twenty-First Century". *The American Economic Review*, 105(5): 48-53.

Polanyi, K. (1944). *The Great Transformation: The Political and Economic Origins of Our Time*. Boston: Beacon Press.

Pooch, M. (2016). Globalization and its Effects. In M. Pooch, DiverCity - *Global Cities as Literary Phenomenon*: Toronto, New York, and Los Angeles in a Globalizing Age (pp. 15-26). Verlag: Transcript.

Powderly, T. V. (1882). The Organization of Labor. *The North American Review*, 135(309): 118-126.

Quillian, L. (2014). Does Segregation Create Winners and Losers? Residential Segregation and Inequality in Educational Attainment. *Social Problems*, 6(3): 402-426.

Rhinehart, L., & McNicholas, C. (2021, April 22). Shortchanged--weak anti-retaliation provisions in the National Labor Relations Act cost workers billions. Economic Policy Institute. Retrieved February 5, 2022, from https://www.epi.org/publication/shortchanged-weak-anti-retaliation-provisions-in-the-national-labor-relations-act-cost-workers-billions/

Rhodes, R. (2006). Old Institutionalism. In R. S. Rhodes, *The Oxford Handbook of Political Institutions* (pp. 90-110). New York: Oxford University Press.

Rhodes, R., Binder, S., & Rockman, B. (2006). *The Oxford Handbook of Political Institutions*. New York: Oxford University Press.

Riesenberg, P. (1992). *Citizenship in the Western Tradition Plato to Rousseau*. Chapel Hill: The University of North Carolina Press.

Rousseau, J., & Cranston, M. (1762; 1968). *The Social Contract*. New York: Penguin Books.

Sachs, J. (2006). The End of Poverty: Economic Possibilities for Our Time. New York: Penguin Press.

Seelye, K. (October 30th, 2015). "In Heroin Crisis, White Families Seek Gentler War on Drugs," *New York Times*: http://www.nytimes.com/2015/10/31/us/heroin-war-on-drugs-parents.html?_r=0: (accessed 06/11/2016).

Shively, P. W. (1972). A Reinterpretation of the New Deal Realignment. The Public *Opinion Quarterly*, 35(4): 621-624.

Siskind, P. (2005). Suburban Growth and Its Discontents, In *The New Suburban History*, by Kevin M. Kruse and Thomas J. Sugrue, 161-182. Chicago: The University of Chicago Press.

Skocpol, T., Finegold, K., & Goldfield, M. (1990). Explaining New Deal Policy. *The American Political Science Review*, 84(4): 1297-1315.

Smith, A. (1986). *The Ethnic Origins of Nations*. Malden: Blackwell.

Smith, A L. (2017). *The American Untouchables America & the Racial Contract*. Wilmington: Vernon Press.

Statistics, U. B. (2022). U.S. Bureau of Labor Statistics. Retrieved on March 3, 2022, from https://www.bls.gov/

Stein, L. (2002). *St. Louis Politics the Triumph of Tradition*, Saint Louis: Missouri Historical Society Press.

Stenner, K. (2005). *The Authoritarian Dynamic*. New York: Cambridge University Press.

Stoesz, D. (1992). The Fall of the industrial City: The Reagan Legacy for Urban Policy. *The Journal of Sociology & Social Welfare*, 19(1): 149-167.

Stolpher, W. F. (1941). Protection and Real Wages. *Review of Economic Studies*, 9(1): 58-73.

Taylor, R. (2010). Kant's Political Religion: The Transparency of Perpetual Peach and the Highest Good. *The Review of Politics*, 72(1): 4-24.

Templeton, A. (1998). Human Races: A genetic and evolutionary perspective, *American Anthropologist*, 100(3): 632-650.

Tong, S. (2020, May 2). Jack Welch's legacy: value for shareholders, but not necessarily for workers. Retrieved February 23, 2022, from Marketplace: https://www.marketplace.org/2020/03/02/jack-welchs-legacy-value-for-share holders-but-not-necessarily-for-workers/

United Electrical, R. A. (1996). Solidarity and Democracy: A leadership guide to UE history. Second Edition. Pittsburgh: United Electrical, Radio, and Machine Workers of America.

United States Bureau of the Census. (1949). *Historical Statistics of the United States 1789-1945: A Supplement to the Statistical Abstract of the United States.*

United States Bureau of the Census. (1935). *Negroes in the United States, 1920-1932*, Washington.

United States Bureau of Labor Statistics. 2021.

United States Center for Disease Control and Prevention. (2016).

United States Census Bureau, H. S. (2021). Historical Statistics of the United States. Retrieved on March 4, 2021, from U.S. Census Bureau: https://www2.census.gov/library/publications/1949/compendia/hist_stats_1789-1945/hist_stats_1789-1945-chE.pdf

United States Department of Education, Office of Educational Research and Improvement. 1993. *120 Years of American Education: A Statistical Potrait.*

United States Department of Justice, Bureau of Justice Statistics. (1986). Historical Corrections Statistics in the United States, 1850-1984.

United States Federal Bureau of Prisons. 2016.

United States Internal Revenue Service. 2022.

Veblen, T. (1899). *The Theory of the Leisure Class*. New York: Oxford University Press.

Vera Institute of Justice, (2016): Retrieved June 12, 2016, from: http://www.vera.org/centers/center-sentencing-and-corrections

Wallerstein, I. (2004). *World-Systems Analysis: An Introduction*. Durham: Duke University Press.

Walton, H. (1997). *African American power and politics: the political context variable*. New York: Columbia University Press.

Warren, H. (1929). *The Gold Coast and the Slum: A Sociological Study of Chicago's Near North Side*. Chicago: The University of Chicago Press, LTD.

Weil, F. (1998). Capitalism and Industrialization in New England, 1815-1845. *The Journal of American History*, 84(14): 1334-1354.

Weisburd, D., Wyckoff, L., Ready, J., Eck, J., Hinkle, J., & Gajewski, J. (2006). Does Crime Just Move Around the Corner? A controlled Study of Spatial

Displacement and Diffusion of Crime Control Benefits, *Criminology*, 44(3): 549-592.

Williamson, S., & Cain, L. P. (2020, January 25). Measuring Slavery in 2020 Dollars. Retrieved February 22, 2021, from Measuring Worth.com: https:// www.measuringworth.com/slavery.php

Wood, A. (1999). *Kant's Ethical Thought.* Cambridge: Cambridge University Press.

Zaller, J. (1992). *The Nature and Origin of Mass Opinion.* Cambridge: Cambridge University Press.

Index

F

federalism, 15, 22, 24, 26, 28, 30,
    31, 32, 37, 46, 50, 87
Federalist 10, 26
feminists, 97
Fenno, 108, 120
Ferguson
    Missouri, 106
feudal system, 100, 101
feudalism, xviii, xix, 12, 13, 15, 20,
    22, 37, 57, 99, 100
FHA, 103
Franklin Roosevelt, 77
French National Front Party, 117,
    118
Fugitive Slave Act, 101
Fukuyama, 15, 121

G

George H.W. Bush, 111, 114
Gerald Ford, 54
Gilbert Padilla, 78
Gompers, 69, 70
Great Depression, 46, 72, 73, 74,
    75, 77, 81, 107
Great Society, 49, 50, 51

H

Herbert Hoover, 72
heroin, 112
heroin epidemic, 111
Hobbes, xiv, 1, 2, 10, 11, 121
Hubert Humphrey, 46, 51, 108

I

Immigration Act of 1917, 45
Immigration Act of 1924, 45

J

James Baldwin, 95
James Madison, 18, 23, 26, 30, 33,
    39
James Watt, 59
jati, 98
Jean Louis Le Pen, 117
Jean-Jacques Rousseau, xiv, 2, 10
Jim Crow, 32, 38, 54, 80, 95, 97, 110
Jimmy Carter, 54
John F. Kennedy, 49
John Locke, xiv, xvi, 1, 2, 122
John Passos, 48
John Saffin, 20, 100
Joyce Appleby, xiii

K

Kansas Nebraska Act, 101
Karl Marx, xx, 11
Kevin Kruse, 105
Kinloch, Missouri, 106
Knights of Labor, 66, 68, 69, 70,
    121, 122

L

Larman Williams, 105
Latinos, 111
Law and Justice Party, 115
Leah Boustan, 105
Lee Atwater, 114
Leninist, 36
Lombard, 117, 122
Lyndon Johnson, 25, 49

M

Magna Carta Libertatum, 5
marginal tax, 75
Marine Le Pen, 118

www.ingramcontent.com/pod-product-compliance
Lightning Source LLC
Chambersburg PA
CBHW062037270326
41929CB00014B/2466